Letters To Young Preachers

Compiled by
Warren Berkley
and

Mark Roberts

Spiritbuilding Publishing

Published by
Spiritbuilding Publishing
15591 N. State Rd. 9, Summitville, IN 46070

Printed in the United States of America

Warren Berkley, Mark Roberts
Letters to Young Preachers
ISBN 9780982981139

Spiritbuilding Publishing

Spiritual "equipment" for the contest of life.

DEDICATED TO

FRANK JAMERSON

Letters to Young Preachers

Table of Contents

Letters to Young Preachers
Introduction

Mark Roberts & Warren Berkley

We live in a society and world that worships youth. Everywhere we look we see advertisements telling us we need to use this product to look younger. The media relentlessly hires only the young and good looking. People pine for their lost youth. All of us know someone who has tried something that utterly fails, like a comb-over or worse, a toupe, to look younger and defeat the inevitable advance of age. We love youth.

Unless we are trying to do something difficult or hard.

No Fortune 500 company's board would excitedly announce they were hiring a 21-year-old "whiz kid" straight out of college to run their corporation. Instead, they parade out a man or woman with a lot of grey in their hair, touting their years of experience, reliability, and wisdom that come from age. Likewise, professional sports franchises don't turn the coaching reins over to a youngster. Instead, a veteran with age who has lived through the turmoil and problems winning and losing at the highest levels can present is tapped to coach the team to a championship. One major league baseball team, the Florida Marlins, even won a World Championship with Jack McKeon steering the team at age 80! When a candidate runs for president he doesn't ask a youth who was just elected to the local town council to come on board as his campaign manager. Again, age, wisdom, and experience are called upon. When we need to do something difficult, whether that is changing the alternator in our car or trying to help a teenager who is rebellious to God, we seek the advice and counsel of those who are older than we are. We don't seek out what a young person says or has to offer simply because they lack the experience that would give them the perspective necessary to offer valuable counsel. So again, when we genuinely need to know, when we are attempting something hard, we want to know what those who are older and more experienced have to say.

The Bible teaches this is the correct approach to life. Repeatedly the Scriptures urge us to listen to those who are older and who simply know about what to do because they have experienced more than we have. Solomon says, "And now, O sons, listen to me, and do not depart from the words of my mouth" (Proverbs 5:7). He goes on to say, "Listen to advice and accept instruction, that you may gain wisdom in the future" (Proverbs 19:20). Some of Paul's most famous words are instructions to two young preachers, Timothy and Titus, to listen to what he teaches them and act accordingly (1 Timothy 2:1; 2 Timothy 1:13; 4:1-2; Titus 2:1). The Bible even shows the folly of young men who will not listen to aged counselors but instead choose to listen to their peers, to their own destruction (see 1 Kings 12:6-14).

Preaching is hard. In our world today there is very little that is easy about it. The local preacher is called upon to wear a variety of different hats, master many skills (some of which are almost contradictory to each other), live nearly perfectly (without being prideful), never offend anyone (while preaching boldly), study a lot (without becoming academic or neglecting visiting), and have a great family life (while still spending a tremendous amount of time with the brethren). It is not easy. Preaching has never been easy but it is surely becoming more difficult than ever, with the demands of technology, the increasing wickedness of the world, and more and more churches expecting more and more of their preacher.

Want a little help? What price would you pay for the venerable and wise counsel of outstanding gospel preachers who have gone before you? If you could sit down for an hour with veteran men who would talk straightforwardly with you about the work of a preacher, the nuts-and-bolts of how to do it better, and give you solid, scriptural advice about your work, how much would you be willing to pay for that hour?

Of course it would seem impossible to get that kind of advice at any price. Who has time to fly all over the country and talk to older preachers? Would those older preachers have time for you if you knocked at their study door?

That is why we put together this book. We asked some of the best and finest preachers of our time to write a letter to a young preacher. Their assignment was to simply think of a young man sitting across their desk and what they would tell him to assist him in being effective in the kingdom. Then they were to write that down. The results were far beyond anything we could have imagined. The wisdom collected here for the reader is powerful, scriptural, and practical. That is an unbeatable combination!

Along with those letters you will also find chapters on the preacher's work written by men who excel in those areas, and can help you do the same. From how to use technology to personal evangelism to personal purity some of the most vital matters in the work of a preacher are covered.

This is, of course, not the first book on preachers and preaching. Many books on preaching deal primarily with the technique of sermon construction and delivery. We are delighted those resources have found a place in the publishing market, and we hope some of these are in your library or on your digital reader. We have read many of those books and we train young preachers in these critical subjects and urge them to read those books. However, in recent years we have observed a growing need for (1) admonitions relating to the character of the preacher and, (2) counsel from older preachers made widely available to the next generation. In *Behind The Preacher's Door*, the first need is addressed. In *Letters To Young Preachers*, we are addressing the second need.

You will find here that our writers address the dangers, but do not neglect the joys of the work. They draw from Scripture first, but as applied through their experience. Their love for the Lord and His servants is the tone and attitude of every word. This book can help you, and it will help every evangelist who takes it seriously and makes definitive changes in their work based on what is advocated here. It is our prayer that this book will take you deeper into the Word, and closer to the Father who loves us, and thus help you to better connect people with that Word and that wonderful Father.

Acknowledgments

Everything we undertake involves the participation of our wives and families. Dena and Paula are the real force behind everything we do, and without them our efforts would never amount to very much at all. Erin Sullivan has become our "go-to" proofreader with suggestions and copy-editing that enables us to get to good final drafts. Carl McMurray and his staff at Spiritbuilding bring the parts of this book all together and apply professional marketing that is critical to getting this book in your hands. Our special thanks to the writers for their early interests in the project, their deadline sensitivity and most of all, the wisdom and thought they brought to the work. Above all, thanks to God for His Son and the message we need to take to the people.

Dear Young Preacher
From Sewell Hall

*But with me it is a very small thing that I should be judged by you
or by a human court. In fact, I do not even judge myself …
He who judges me is the Lord"* (1 Corinthians 4:3-4).

I am thankful for you. I see a large number of young men who appear to me to be preaching for love of the Lord and love of souls, and I trust that you are one of them. I do not write this because I feel particularly wise. Instead, I am aware of some of the mistakes I have made, and I have observed the mistakes of others and the consequences that followed. I do not want you to make the same mistakes, and that is the reason for this letter.

Some Things You Must Do

"Take heed to yourself and to the doctrine. Continue in them, for in doing this you will save both yourself and those who hear you" (1 Timothy 4:16). Only in this one matter are you to think of yourself first. It is not likely that you will raise "those who hear you" to a higher spiritual level than you attain. Jesus is your example and He "began both to do and teach" (Acts 1:1). "Walking in truth" must come before "speaking the truth." It is hypocrisy to preach a higher standard than you are, at least, trying diligently to attain. "Keep yourself pure" (1 Timothy 5:22).

Taking heed to your doctrine (teaching) is also essential. Style is important, but much more important is the content of your preaching. Be sure to obtain it from diligent and daily study of the Scripture—not from "church of Christ tradition," other preachers, religious papers, uninspired books, college professors, commentaries, or the Internet.

These may help you understand and cross-reference Scripture, but Scripture is your only dependable source of truth. Truth never changes and it must never be silenced or compromised to achieve political correctness or audience acceptance. Your responsibility is to change sinners—not accommodate them, and God's truth is your weapon for changing them (2 Corinthians 10:5).

Make sure you keep the proper emphasis in your preaching. Salvation is in Christ, not in being associated with a particular group of people, regardless of what may be on the sign in front of their meeting place. Those who are in Christ will seek fellowship with others who are in Christ, but it is the relationship with Christ that saves. Salvation is "by grace through faith," not by simply doing the right things. Just as faith without works is dead (James 2:26), even so works without faith is dead (Hebrews 11:6).

Study diligently each lesson you intend to present. God expects you to make the most of every opportunity to teach His Word. He deserves your careful preparation and so does your audience. In addition, spend time in study and prayer for your own personal edification. We expect others to do this, why not preachers?

If you are not married now, be very careful whom you marry. Your companion will make a major difference in your effectiveness as a gospel preacher. If she is a dedicated Christian and a good example of godly womanhood, if she is hospitable, if she can be content with a modest or even sub-standard lifestyle, if she is willing to go with you wherever you feel that the Lord would have you go, she will be a blessing. If not, she will be a hindrance.

Be sure to show gratitude for financial support that brethren give you and for every kindness they show you. Do not be constantly asking for more. Every preacher would do well to duplicate Paul's attitude demonstrated in his response to the gifts of the Philippians. While revealing contentment in his circumstances, he expressed genuine appreciation for what their gifts represented and rejoiced in the fruit that would abound to their account (Philippians 4:10-18).

If a congregation where you are preaching feels they need a change, leave without causing a problem. If you have a right to initiate a change in your relationship with a church, they have the same right. If a major doctrinal issue is involved, this might make a difference; but if it is simply a personal matter, you will do yourself, your family, and the church a favor by leaving without murmuring. The unity of a church is more important than your personal pride or your family's convenience. By showing a proper attitude you can avoid embittering your family against the church.

Some Things You Must Not Do

Do not preach for money or for prestige or favor of men. It is not wrong to be supported (1 Corinthians 9:6-14), and if you stand for what is right, good people will usually encourage and honor you. But if your goals are carnal in nature, you will be constantly tempted both to compromise the truth and to choose selfishly your field of labor. Determine to preach in the place where you believe that God would have you preach. Preaching for large congregations is not wrong, but this is not something to be sought; it is rather a door to be entered if it appears to offer the greatest opportunity for service. At the same time, some preachers need to be serving where Christ has not been named (Romans 15:20). You may sometime have to support yourself with secular work in order to preach where you are needed, but if this should prove to be necessary, you will be following in the footsteps of some of God's greatest evangelists. Just as Paul had a backup source of income, there are young men now who are taking training in secular fields that will allow them to follow the example of Paul.

Do not jeopardize your influence by unguarded association with women. Beware especially of privately counseling those with marital problems. Even in efforts to convert one who is lost, it is best to have another person present. One preacher we knew insisted on a glass window in his office door at the church building, and another who was married had a rule never to ride in a car alone with a woman to whom he was not related. Such rules may seem extreme in our increasingly casual society, but those two preachers were never suspected of immorality. Some who have succumbed to temptation would have avoided sin if they had observed such rules. "Therefore let him who thinks he stands take heed lest he fall" (1 Corinthians 10:12). Even if you keep yourself pure, you need to be able to prove your innocence if false charges are made. We must "have regard for what is honorable, not only in the sight of the Lord, but also in the sight of men" (2 Corinthians 8:21).

"Do not be carried about with various and strange doctrines" (Hebrews 13:9). Independent thinking does not require you to adopt some strange doctrine or scheme of interpretation. One is just as dependent on what he has been taught if he automatically rejects it as if he automatically accepts it. "Test all things; hold fast what is good" (1 Thessalonians 5:21). If in your independent study you feel that you have discovered some new truth, "test" it first with knowledgeable brethren who may help you see any fallacy there may be in your thinking. Only when your discovery is thoroughly tested and essential to "the faith" should it be preached. On the other hand, if you find that what you have been taught is true, thank God and "contend earnestly for the faith which was once for all delivered to the saints" (Jude 3).

Avoid expressing strong opinions on political and social issues. When you "contend earnestly for the faith," you will alienate enough people without generating additional contention over matters of spiritual indifference. Jesus did not join in protest against the atrocities of Pilate (Luke 13:1-3), nor did Paul pen one word in criticism of the notoriously corrupt Roman government. Rather he wrote, "I have become all things to all men, that I might by all means save some" (1 Corinthians 9:22).

Do not abuse the freedom you have in the use of your time. "See then that you walk circumspectly, not as fools but as wise, redeeming the time, because the days are evil" (Ephesians 5:15-16). Too many preachers have done foolish things because they had time for which they were not accountable to anyone. Availability of the Internet can encourage a waste of time in arguing about "foolish and unlearned questions" (2 Timothy 2:23) or in pursuing "foolish and harmful lusts which drown men in destruction and perdition" (1 Timothy 6:9). If you have nothing pressing you otherwise, get out and find someone to teach.

Do not take too seriously the kind things people say regarding your preaching. Just as it is considered polite to commend a hostess for the meal she has provided, many feel it is common courtesy to say, "Enjoyed your sermon." Realize that the praise that goes beyond this is often from people given by nature to flattery. "But with me it is a very small thing that I should be judged by you or by a human court. In fact, I do not even judge myself … He who judges me is the Lord" (1 Corinthians 4:3-4).

Strive For Balance

Balance is one of the most difficult qualities to maintain. All of us tend to give priority to things we enjoy doing over things we need to do. We must strive for balance in the following areas.

Between study and personal contacts: No one wants a doctor who never studies his medical books, but neither would we want one who only studies and seldom treats or operates on a patient. Preachers need to study, but they also need to know the people to whom they preach. Visitation increases one's influence and personalizes one's preaching, especially when it is visiting those who are sick, bereaved, or burdened in some special way. Without visitation, preaching tends to become academic and scholarly rather than practical.

Between preaching "publicly and from house to house": Paul did both (Acts 20:20). I can remember a time when non-Christians would come to hear public preaching and search "the Scriptures daily to find out whether these things were so" (Acts 17:11). Large numbers were converted by such preaching. Public preaching has not lost its power, but it has lost its audience of unbelievers. Preaching is still powerful for Christians but, as a rule, if unbelievers are to be reached, they must be taught on a personal level in some venue other than a church building. It is a preacher's responsibility to find ways of contacting such people to bring them to the Lord.

Between preaching on practice and attitudes: When religiously mistaken people attended our meetings, they had usually been well taught on such things as attitudes, morality, and the authority of Jesus and Scripture. So we preached often on baptism, rightly dividing the word, the errors of denominationalism, instrumental music, etc. One of my most admired young preachers recently wrote, "Realistically, these issues are not the ones we tend to struggle with anyway. How many of you will be tempted to play an instrument when you assemble this Sunday? How many of you will have to resist bringing hamburgers and coke to the Lord's Supper table? I would guess none." He may be correct in saying that "these issues are not the ones we tend to struggle with," now. But what about the future if we do not teach on such things?

When I was his age, I would never have dreamed that "churches of Christ" might someday be using instrumental music, building gymnasiums, allowing women to preach, and having the Lord's Supper on Saturday night, but these things are now being practiced by some. And by whom? By those who assumed everyone knew the truth on such matters and ceased teaching on them. Meanwhile a generation grew up that did not know the truth, and new converts were attracted by appeals other than the unique and scriptural practices of the Lord's church. Consequently they did not know the error of these unscriptural things and began to practice them. Preaching on loving one another and worship from the heart is indeed timely, and we may have neglected such teaching in the past. But, "These you ought to have done, without leaving the others undone" (Matthew 23:23). We might be surprised to know how many in our audience see no wrong in instrumental music and other innovations. If we do not teach repeatedly on these things, a generation will arise that will accept them.

Between the Old and New Testaments: We assume that Christians know the New Testament and so we may spend a disproportionate amount of time in the Old Testament in order to maintain freshness. We may also feel our own weakness in the Old Testament and choose to teach from it in order to learn more about it ourselves. Study of the Old Testament is valuable, but while "the law was given through Moses, grace and truth came through Jesus Christ" (John 1:17). "God, who at various times and in various ways spoke in time past to the fathers by the prophets, has in these last days spoken to us by His Son" (Hebrews 1:1-2). The purpose of the Old Testament is "to bring us to Christ, that we might be justified by faith" (Galatians 3:24). It should be studied to help us understand the New, but people need to major in the gospels, Acts, and the epistles before getting deeply involved in the intricacies of Old Testament law and prophecy.

Between rational and emotional: We live in an age in which feeling dominates. People love emotional highs: scary movies, tear jerking stories, exciting roller-coasters, violent sports, throbbing music—anything that stirs the emotions. We are not too keen on things that make us think. The gospel is rational; it appeals to the intellect. When the gospel is explained and understood it will produce emotional responses: sorrow for sin, gratitude for grace, hope of heaven, etc., and these are important to faithfulness. Many, however, want to skip the rational and get to the emotional. Preachers are tempted to accommodate such desires and to spend more time telling stories than citing Scripture. Emotion that is produced by any other means than teaching is emotionalism. Those converted by emotionalism with little knowledge of the truth "have no root, who believe for a while and in time of temptation fall away" (Luke

8:13). A careful exposition of doctrine as contained in the gospels and in the epistles will not have the popular appeal that many preachers seek to generate, but it is the only foundation for strong faith.

Between rebuking and exhorting: To preach the word, one must "Convince, rebuke, exhort, with all longsuffering and teaching" (2 Timothy 4:2). Some preachers seem to know only one part of this— rebuking and condemning. Others exhort effectively but are "too nice" to condemn sin. Balanced preaching does both. Actually, rebuke will have little value unless it is balanced with exhortation and encouragement. Note Paul's expressions of love and confidence in addressing the church in Corinth before getting to the rebukes that he had in mind (1 Corinthians 1:4-9). There is good in almost every individual and congregation, and due note should be taken of it if we are to rebuke what is wrong. And such rebuke is essential from time to time.

Between information and application: A popular speech book published some years ago suggested a series of questions a speaker should imagine the audience asking. For example, when he has presented considerable information, he should imagine their saying, "So what?" I must confess that I have listened to several sermons that ended, leaving me asking, "So what?" While the first part of such epistles as Romans, Galatians, Ephesians, and Colossians is given over to instruction in doctrine, the latter part is answering the question, "So what?" If we cannot think of practical applications of a message we present, we should find some other message. People need something to take home with them that will make a difference.

Between time for family and time for the work of an evangelist: Preachers have made mistakes in both directions. One preacher neglects his family to the point that his wife and children feel that he cares for everyone else but them. Another takes advantage of the fact that he does not have to punch a clock and spends far more time with his family than the average father can spend. If the church is not to fund education, neither should it employ a preacher to give full time to homeschooling. Some time so spent is not wrong, but it must not dominate his schedule. A family man may not be able to "warn everyone night and day" to the extent that Paul did (Acts 20:31), but if he is being fully supported by a congregation, he should be giving as much time to gospel work as other men give to their secular responsibilities. After all, whatever they do for the Lord is in addition to the 40 hours they spend on the job. Why should a preacher not spend more than 40 hours in gospel work? One thing that can make his absences from the family beneficial to them is to keep them aware that any sacrifice they have to make is for the Lord.

Conclusion

Writing these things reminds me of how far short I have come of being what I wanted to be as an evangelist. Whatever I have done right is due to the good example and instruction of my father and mother, the encouragement and guidance of godly men and women, and my own feeble efforts to learn and follow the instructions of Scripture. God's Word is your infallible guide and to whatever extent you find my thoughts and suggestions in harmony with it "commit these to faithful men who will be able to teach others also" (2 Timothy 2:2). This is God's plan for the continued preaching of truth, even after you and I have gone to our reward.

How to Build Your Knowledge Base
By Dan Petty

"Be diligent to present yourself approved to God as a workman who does not need to be ashamed, accurately handling the word of truth" (2 Timothy 2:15). *There is simply no other way.*

Preaching is teaching, and teaching is imparting knowledge. The young man who makes the commitment to preach the gospel is taking on a great responsibility because the knowledge he sets out to teach others has eternal implications. But no person can teach what he himself does not know.

What does it take to build and maintain your personal foundation of knowledge? Perhaps the most important ingredient is what Paul prescribed for Timothy: "nourished on the words of the faith and of the sound doctrine" (1 Timothy 4:6).

It is imperative for the young preacher to start early to establish attitudes, develop habits, and formulate plans that will help him build a foundation of knowledge. Here are some basic steps to help guide you in that process.

Make a plan for regular reading and study. Learning that is beneficial does not just happen without deliberate forethought and preparation. Wilbur M. Smith, in *The Minister in His Study*, observed that the preacher who is about to begin a lifelong study of the Bible and related subjects must make four preliminary basic decisions: (1) how much time he will devote to study every day; (2) the subjects he is going to study through the years; (3) what books he is going to read; and (4) how he is going to preserve the material he reads for future, easy reference (10-16). Smith's excellent discussion suggests the vital importance of planning a program of personal study.

Just what such a plan should look like will vary for each individual since we all have different backgrounds, abilities, and interests. I would suggest the young preacher start out by looking at study methods others have developed. A good place to begin might be Wilbur M. Smith's *Profitable Bible Study*. Smith discusses several proven methods for personal Bible study and offers suggestions for more effective study. Irving L. Jensen's *Independent Bible Study* is an excellent guidebook that focuses on studying the biblical text inductively and analytically. *Creative Bible Study* by Lawrence O. Richards is designed as a handbook for personal or group study, and emphasizes a God-centered, practical approach to Bible study. These and other works may prove useful as you begin to find for yourself the method of study that works best. Whatever plan you develop, the important thing is to have a plan.

A plan of Bible study for the young preacher may involve various approaches. A methodical book-by-book approach will be useful when surveying the Bible. A historical approach is important for learning the chronology of the Bible as well as the causes and consequences of the great events in the story. There is value in studying the great themes or doctrines of the Bible, especially the central theme of redemption and the Messiah. A biographical approach enables you to study the great movers in the story of the Bible, as well as providing practical character studies. The study of the original languages of Scripture, though certainly not essential to understanding the Bible or teaching others, can enhance your ability to study the text.

In addition to the methodical study of the Bible, your study may also include subjects related to the Bible. History, for example, is important since the message of Scripture is the story of God's people in history. Some knowledge of ancient history helps provide a broader historical context for the history recorded in the Bible. The history of Christianity, or church history, is the story of the church through the ages since the first century and provides a context for understanding the variety of religious beliefs and churches in existence today. The study of apologetics, or Christian evidences, is another field of study that is important in equipping the young preacher to defend the faith, and build it in others.

Select your reading and study materials. Not only is a plan necessary for fruitful study, but the young preacher should begin developing a plan for acquiring books and other study materials. A preacher's library should be thought of as tools of his trade. Care ought to be given to what tools he looks for. A plan for the choice of books is as important as is a plan for the use of those books.

Michael Weed offers several suggestions in *The Minister and His Work* for the preacher as he builds his library, the most important of which is simply to keep a list of desired books (41). Of course, many factors determine what goes into the list and how the list is prioritized. The young preacher needs to choose wisely those materials that he needs most and that will profit him most. Again, interests vary, so the choice of books for your library is a personal matter.

Knowing what books are available and what they offer is an important part of the process. There are several types or categories of books that you will need to consider when compiling your list, including Bible translations, concordances, lexicons, word studies, introductions, dictionaries, encyclopedias, atlases, Bible geography, history, church history, restoration history, theology, and apologetics.

Once again, there are several good discussions available that can help the young preacher become better acquainted with the many resources that he might consider. Most of these arrange the books under basic categories. One of the most thorough and scholarly studies of this kind is Frederick Danker's *Multi-Purpose Tools for Bible Study*. Danker's work is a reliable guide to the foundational texts of biblical study that includes help on how to use those tools. Smith's *The Minister in His Study*, though dated, discusses the basic books in the preacher's library, arranged according to basic categories of study. In *Profitable Bible Study*, you will find a chapter on "Basic Books (and a Few Others) for the Bible Student's Library." Smith's listing in this volume is also arranged according to fields of study, and includes a discussion of some principles that guided him in his choices.

Other ways of knowing about what books to consider acquiring, especially new ones, include reading book reviews in religious journals. Subscribing to publishers' catalogs or joining book clubs are good ways to keep up with what's being published. The Internet, with sites such as *Amazon.com* and *Abebooks.com*, provides ample means of searching for new and used books and getting the best prices. And don't forget to ask others, especially older preachers whom you respect, to suggest good books.

Religious journals can provide a good source of reading material in the form of articles on specific subjects. Journals published by brethren offer articles written mostly by other preachers. There are also journals from denominational publishers as well as scholarly journals dealing with biblical studies.

In this age of digital information, any consideration of a library must also include the wide array of materials available in digital format. There are several good Bible study software programs available that have much to offer. Among the more well-known and proven are *BibleWorks*, *Logos*, *PC Study Bible*, and *QuickVerse*. All of these programs and others have features such as multiple Bible translations and search capabilities. Most include packages with hundreds of reference works that would cost thousands of dollars if purchased as individual volumes. Some place greater emphasis on the study of the Greek and Hebrew text than others. In addition to Bible study software, many good reference works are available on CD or downloadable from the Internet.

The Internet offers many good resources for your study in areas ranging from the Bible to theology to church history. *The NET Bible*

(Biblical Studies Press) is a good example of a site dedicated to Bible study. The *Christian Classics Ethereal Library* focuses on classical writings from the history of Christianity, as does the *Internet Christian Library* (ICLNet). And there are some very good websites provided by brethren, such as the *Biblical Studies Info Page* by Ferrell Jenkins. Many religious journals are also available online.

But a word of warning is warranted at this point. While there is much good material on the Internet, there is far more that is of poor quality. Of course any resource, whether in print or in digital format, must be weighed and judged critically for its value and credibility. That is especially true with material you will find on the Internet, so be discriminating. Any good website will provide publication information, and you should always consider that.

A final word, before moving on, is that there is little value in acquiring books if those books are not opened, read, and studied. Have a plan for your study, and then work the plan!

Keep your study focused on the Bible. There is value in reading, and reading widely. The broad study of subjects about the Bible, Bible history and geography, religion, church history, apologetics, and other Bible-related matters can only enrich your knowledge of the Bible and of the gospel message you preach. There is value in reading subjects not directly related to the Bible. Such wide reading will contribute to a broader perspective about life, the world, and society that can enhance your ability to relate the gospel to the lives of those you teach.

But how vital it is to keep the study of the Bible itself at the center! There is simply no substitute for careful, methodical study of the text of Scripture in context. The Bible is the Word of God. Every young preacher should take to heart Paul's admonition to Timothy: "All Scripture is inspired by God and profitable for teaching, for reproof, for correction, for training in righteousness; so that the man of God may be adequate, equipped for every good work" (2 Timothy 3:16-17).

Relate your study to your preaching and teaching. A systematic plan of preaching can help make your study more profitable. Preaching in series is not only beneficial to the congregation, but also provides the preacher a plan for careful study of a biblical theme or a book of the Bible.

Expository preaching can be especially rewarding. There are several advantages to engaging in a systematical exposition of a book of the Bible as opposed to topical preaching. It lends itself to a more careful consideration of the context, letting the Bible speak for itself. It can offer a more "even" approach to preaching, covering themes and passages that otherwise might be neglected. Preaching through an entire section of God's word enables one to see that book of the Bible as a whole and how its parts fit together. For the preacher, this kind of preaching is an opportunity to engage in a careful, in-depth study that can help him develop a greater appreciation of God's word.

Of course, preaching in series may also include enriching studies on biblical themes, character studies, word studies, and the like. In any case, when the preacher plans his preaching in this manner, he not only provides a good, balanced spiritual diet for his listeners, but he helps himself. When he knows where he is going with his sermons for a month or more at a time, he has made an initial decision about what and where to study.

The same is true, of course, of the preacher's studies in preparation for a Bible class or extended study. As a young preacher, you should see the decision to spend a quarter or more teaching a class on Romans, for example, as an opportunity to engage in a careful personal study of the subject that will broaden and deepen your own knowledge of the subject.

One additional benefit of planning your study in relation to your preaching and teaching is that it helps you keep your study practical and useful in nature. Study can become purely academic or intellectual in nature if we are not careful. Building your study around your preaching and teaching will help you keep your head out of the clouds and your feet on the ground.

Take advantage of available educational opportunities. There are many educational opportunities—both formal and informal—available to help young preachers not only establish a base of knowledge but continue to grow.

College training of the right kind can be a profitable investment of time and resources that will serve the minister throughout life. We expect those in various secular professions or callings to be well-prepared and well-informed in their field. I believe the preacher of the gospel should be no less prepared. I would encourage every young man who wants to preach to get a college education, and if possible, one that focuses on the study of the Bible. For those who are unable to attend college or take a traditional college course, there are increasing opportunities to take college courses through online distance learning formats.

Young preachers should consider the "preacher-training" programs that some local churches provide. Sometimes described as "internship" arrangements, these programs give the young preacher a one-to-two-year experience of working under the oversight of elders and the guidance of an older preacher. These experiences provide valuable practical experience in sermon preparation, preaching, teaching, and evangelism, while engaging in a planned program of guided Bible study. In such a setting you can establish good habits of work and study that will help you throughout your life.

There are also less formal educational opportunities for the young preacher who wants to keep learning. You might have the opportunity to spend time studying with an older, more experienced preacher who lives nearby. In some locales various preachers in the area might meet together periodically for a Bible class or study group. You can gain much from these associations and study sessions. College lectureships, Bible lectureships conducted by local churches, and the like are great opportunities to be spiritually replenished while continuing to grow in knowledge.

Decide how you will preserve what you read and learn for easy future reference. Very few people have the ability to remember everything they have ever read. So it is important for you to decide how you are going to keep the material you think is worth saving, and to do so in a way that you may easily draw upon those resources. For most people this is accomplished by some kind of filing system.

Various filing methods have been tried, and you will find books that recommend one or the other. Wilbur Smith in *The Minister in His Study* (82-94) discusses four major methods for preserving material we may someday wish to consult or use: (1) wide-margin or loose-leaf Bibles for recording brief notes on the biblical text; (2) notebooks; (3) file folders; and (4) card indexes. Notebooks can be useful for compiling and arranging material on a book of the Bible or biblical subject. This can be especially useful for material used in teaching. File folders might be used for collecting articles or other printed material. They are usually classified alphabetically, textually (based on the books of the Bible), or by subject. Card indexes, classified as textual or alphabetical, can be used for recording references to material you have studied on a specific biblical text or topic, or illustrations that might be useful for sermon development.

The computer can be a wonderful tool for preserving and filing information and in some cases makes the older methods obsolete. The use of index cards, for example, is probably largely unnecessary when you can create a database, scan material, or simply create a document that can then be easily stored, organized, and searched for future use.

The important point is that whatever system is used, you ought to begin early to decide how you will preserve and file the material you have studied and read, and be diligent in sticking with the system. As time passes, the care you put into this effort will pay rich dividends.

Don't neglect your personal devotional life. It is easy to allow your study to become a purely intellectual activity. This may occur if we focus all our study on the doctrinal truths of Scripture, as critically important as those truths are to our faith, without considering the practical and personal implications of those truths. We may allow our preaching to become just an intellectual exercise of debate arguments on opposing sides of an issue. Your study will have become imbalanced if it is nothing more than an academic approach.

Much of your study will be necessary, of course, because you have a sermon to prepare or a class to teach. You might engage in study because you have an article to write or a bulletin to publish. You might even be engaged in developing Bible class material or writing a book.

Begin now practicing the discipline of personal, daily devotion. Paul said he practiced such self-discipline "so that, after I have preached to others, I myself will not be disqualified" (1 Corinthians 9:27). He urged Timothy to do the same: "Take pains with these things; be absorbed in them, so that your progress will be evident to all. Pay close attention to yourself and to your teaching; persevere in these things, for as you do this you will ensure salvation both for yourself and for those who hear you" (1 Timothy 4:15-16).

In conclusion, be passionate about learning, disciplined in your habits, and diligent in your study. Commit yourself now, as a young preacher, to be a life-long student. "Be diligent to present yourself approved to God as a workman who does not need to be ashamed, accurately handling the word of truth" (2 Timothy 2:15). There is simply no other way.

Works Consulted

1. Danker, Frederick W. *Multi-Purpose Tools for Bible Study*. rev. ed. Minneapolis: Fortress, 1993.
2. Jensen, Irving L. *Independent Bible Study: Using the Analytical Chart and the Inductive Method*. Chicago: Moody, 1963.

3. Richards, Lawrence O. *Creative Bible Study*. Grand Rapids: Zondervan, 1971.
4. Smith, Wilbur M. *Profitable Bible Study*. 2nd rev. ed. Grand Rapids: Baker, 1963.
5. Smith, Wilbur M. *The Minister in His Study*. Chicago: Moody, 1973.
6. Weed, Michael R., ed. *The Minister and His Work*. Austin, Tex.: Sweet, 1970.

How to Build Trust with Members
By Wilson Adams

In your opinion, what is the secret to preaching?" asked the young preacher conducting the phone interview. I wasn't sure why he was calling me unless it had something to do with the fact that the "older" preacher training him had occupied the desk across the hall from mine about fifteen years ago. Oddly enough, he had a similar assignment. "First of all, the secret to effective preaching is no secret," I suggested. "It's simple, really *love the people*."

Isn't that profound?

Sometimes I am asked to recommend books that are helpful when it comes to preaching. Some books focus on honing homiletical skills, others deal with the nuts and bolts of ministry, and still others focus entirely on the importance of connecting rather than merely communicating (some preachers have to say something while others have something to say). Each has points worthy of validation and application.

There are four books, however, that are the quintessential reference books for preaching. In fact, I imagine you have them in your library already. Here they are: *Matthew, Mark, Luke, and John*. If you are serious about preaching the gospel, then focus on Jesus, the greatest preacher of all. Jesus has a perfect grasp of hermeneutics, homiletics, and the ability to connect truth to reality. His preaching was simple, yet profound. He could connect with Pharisee and farmer, men and women, older folks and children. He (1) started where they were; (2) gave them good news; (3) related truth to life; (4) spoke in an interesting yet simple way; and (5) wasn't afraid to call for a life-changing decision. Through it all, His love for people was transparent in everything He did and said. Then again, that's why He came (John 3:16).

It's All About the People

Jesus proved once and for all time that ministers minister with a small "m." He came to serve and not be served (Mark 10:45). And when He said, "You shall know the truth and the truth shall set you free" the "you" is *people*. And because truth is for the benefit of people, preaching (the dissemination of truth) is about the people.

Before a preacher can preach, he has to know the needs of the people. A preacher that doesn't take the time to know "the folks" and/or ignores their life situations will not build trust with anyone. After all, how do you "reprove, rebuke, exhort …" (2 Timothy 4:2) if your heart is not with the people? Sure, you *can* do those things, but you won't do them effectively. The old saying is true: *People don't care how much you know until they know how much you care.* Return to those four books about preaching and see if Jesus wasn't the Master at connecting those dots.

Jesus erased generational lines like a baseball player kicks away the chalk lines around home plate. It's easy to love people with whom you share common stations in life: age, kids, hobbies, etc. The Jesus-like preacher, however, reaches out to everyone and without favoritism. He loves the older folks and touches them with care and concern. And he does the same for the younger ones. Last year I watched a little girl come running down the aisle at the Temple Terrace, Florida church building and into the arms of a kneeling Don Truex. It was a night when the building was packed and people from across the country were in attendance. For a few moments, however, my old college roommate fixed his attention completely on that little one. *"Send the children away for they are bothersome,"* complained the disciples. Not on your life! In fact, Mark records a touching scene that every preacher needs to note: "And He took them [children] in His arms and began blessing them" (10:16).

If you want a measure of a gospel preacher's effectiveness, look to see the attention he gives to those who don't get much. Is that not one of the greatest lessons Jesus taught us about preaching?

Love Everyone

Someone other than me counted the number of times in the New Testament when we are told to *love* and came up with the number: 55. One is enough, 55 seems to shout an unmistakable emphasis. If we don't love people, nothing else matters! John said, "The one who does not love does not know God, for God is love" (1 John 4:8).

Every congregation thinks they are loving (if you don't believe it, ask them). Then again, maybe that's because the folks that think they are unloving aren't there! Loving people you like is easy; loving people that you may not naturally be drawn to is not so easy.

Some churches mistake the lack of a crowd with being biblical (which in some places *does* have merit). On the other hand, it may bespeak volumes about their lack of love to reach out to others. I have observed through the years this simple truth: *Some churches don't have a crowd because they don't want one!* They say all the right things, "We're glad you're here" or, "Stick around after services so we can get to know you," but their body language and lack of kindness says the very opposite. And by the way, the size of a church has nothing to do with their love. Some of the most unloving groups I have witnessed were small churches while some of the most loving were large. I have seen the opposite, too. How does this relate to God's preacher? Because the preacher, of all people, must set the Jesus-example by exuding a climate of warmth. He sets the tone for the congregation.

Creating an Atmosphere

When we planted a new church in White House, Tennessee in the spring of 2001, we met for the first two years in a middle school cafeteria. In addition to hauling out song books, chairs, podium, and communion table each week, we set out trees and plants all around the makeshift auditorium. Why? Because we wanted to create an atmosphere that said to everyone walking through the doors, *something is alive in here!* Preacher colleague, you must be alive in here!

I say this with hesitancy for fear some will take it to an extreme, yet I say it with candor. It is more important for you to arrive early and talk with the elderly ladies (they always come early) than it is to spend time getting your PowerPoint ready. Churches could use more of the former and less of the latter. I have driven to hear brothers preach the gospel only to see them secluded behind the podium perfecting their presentation when they should be walking and talking to the people. We don't need more techno-geeks—we need gospel preachers that know how to come down and connect with the folks. Do you want to build trust with members? That's how.

Brother, long before you ever open your mouth to preach, people have sized you up with one simple question: *Does he care about me?* You can preach all the book, chapter, and verse sermons you wish (and you must!), but until you join that with common courtesy, warmth, and kindness, your words will not connect. May I remind you that one of the qualifications for preaching in 2 Timothy 2:24 is kindness? "And the Lord's bondservant … must be kind to all."

You may argue that kindness is a duty of all Christians. That's true. You may argue that it's not the preacher's job to shake hands and be friendly any more than anyone else. True again.

You may argue that we must exercise care not to develop the clergy-laity distinctions so prevalent in denominations where preachers reside on pedestals. I got it. But hear me clearly: No one in the congregation has more visibility than the gospel preacher. It just goes with the territory. And unlike the denominations and their pedestal clergy, you have taken on a work that causes you to step up by stepping down. God calls you to step down to where the people are and connect with them on a personal level. Jesus wasn't a statue in a cathedral nor was He an untouchable teacher on an elevated pulpit. He connected with people on a personal level and made each one feel as if they were the most important person in the world. And to Him, they were. Unless you do the same, you will never build trust.

Four Keys to Trust-Building

- *Memorize names.* Learning names shows you care. People have a name and they like to hear you speak it. I drive across town to the same cleaners each week for one simple reason: they know my name and call it as soon as I walk in the door. I rent vehicles occasionally from the local Enterprise Rental-Car Company because the manager takes the time to step away from his desk, shake my hand, and say, "Mr. Adams, we appreciate your business." It makes a difference. Few things are more important in a preacher's work than to know the people to whom he preaches. And that starts with knowing their names.

- *Greet people before and after.* Assemblies are *not* the time for private meetings (that goes for elders, too). Assemblies *are* the time to connect with as many people as you can. Greeting warmly and with affection is a skill you must develop. You can argue against his politics and/or personal life, but President Bill Clinton was adept at talking one on one. Phil Ford, an elder in the church at East Shelby in Memphis and a business owner in West Memphis, Arkansas, knows Clinton well. He said, "Bill Clinton has a way of greeting each one as if they are a lifelong friend." That is a high compliment and a rarity. Reagan did it. Mike Huckabee does it. Tony Dungy and John Maxwell do it. Preacher friend, work on being more personable in your one-on-one conversations. Give the one to whom you speak your undivided attention. Make them feel special because they *are* special. Oh yes, re-read the four recommended books on preaching and you'll see that Jesus did it better than anyone.

- *Touch people.* Jesus gave people more than words; He gave them His touch. "And moved with compassion, He stretched out His hand and touched him" (Mark 1:41). When I go to the hospital, I touch people. When I greet people, I touch them. Some folks aren't huggers (and you'll know who they are), but most are. And your hug may be the only one they get! Behind every smile is a hidden hurt that your hug may heal. It's essential, however, on this point that you understand boundaries. This must be a familial touch (hug) and nothing more. It's an area requiring much discernment and wisdom and when in doubt, don't.

- *Use a warm and personal style in writing notes.* I have always been big on note writing. E-mail is quick and sometimes effective, but nothing takes the place of the old-fashioned hand-written, USPS-stamped note. While doing local church work, I would write such a note to each member and child once per year—usually coinciding with birthdays. A couple hours of the day, early in my week, would usually be all the time I needed to carry out the assignment. It's amazing how many would greet me at the next assembly to express appreciation for their note. Just a cup of cold water in the form of encouraging words written on a simple piece of paper will go far in building trust.

"But I'm Busy!"

I hope so. Preaching is "work" and hard work at that. "Be diligent to present yourself approved to God as a *workman* …" (2 Timothy 2:15). "Do the *work* of an evangelist" (4:5). "We must work the works of Him who sent Me" (John 9:4). Preachers are like everyone else—there are good ones and not-so-good-ones. However, there is no "Angie's List" to grade preachers. The truth of, "You shall know them by their fruit," certainly applies. People will know if you work hard or hardly work.

My friend, Terry Slack, called last week from a Dallas-area hospital where he was sitting with a family during surgery. He was leaving there and going to another hospital to sit with yet another family facing the same ordeal. It would be sometime in the afternoon before he reached his desk. He didn't complain although he knew it would be a long day. It's what preachers do.

There are some things you can't schedule and must schedule around. And that's one of them. When people face crisis-points in life, *go!* And while your words of comfort may not even be remembered on such occasions, one thing will be remembered: You showed up! Sure, you can't be all things to all people all of the time. Equally sure is the fact that people may expect more of you than you can give. But do your best to connect with hurting people at life-defining moments.

One preacher argued that hospital "visiting" was the work of every Christian and not the "job" of the preacher. I get his point although it is a "so-what?" argument. So, go as a Christian. Since the Lord has blessed you with flexible hours and daytime opportunities, *go!* And the next time you preach a lesson about Jesus, maybe some in the audience will reflect upon an example of how your life matches His.

Sermon preparation, class work, articles to write for the bulletin, PowerPoint slides to make (see, I'm not 100% opposed), personal study and reading time, answering the phone, writing notes of encouragement, one-on-one studies, people dropping by on their day off (which isn't your day off), and visiting the sick and bereaved reminds each of us of the "work" of God's preacher. And it's a work that is never done. Like Jesus, who went to bed each night with unfinished business, we, too, have to prioritize our time. Did He not arise early some days to seek solace and seclusion with the Father (Mark 1:35; Luke 5:16)? Perhaps you need to begin earlier, too. It's amazing how much work you can accomplish before 9:00 a.m. (when the phone begins to ring), if you start "early in the morning while it is still dark."

One more thing… No one was ever busier than Jesus. If you want to get a grasp on time-management, study how He set His priorities in those four "How To" books mentioned previously.

Don't Forget Your Family

It's essential to remember that while you're building trust with members, it's easy for members of your own family to go lacking. You will need time each week to walk away from work and relax. Don't be afraid to take it and, if any elders read this, don't be afraid to enforce it. Monday has always been "our" day. Terry Slack, whom I mentioned earlier, grabs Thursday for the day of devotion to his wife. Regardless, you have to have a day. Or she does. Or they do. It's the day in which my wife/family gets all my attention. It's nothing for Julie and I to sip morning coffee at Panera Bread until morning turns into lunch. Or maybe she wants to go shopping. Or maybe she doesn't want to go anywhere. Whatever the case, prioritize time each week to build trust with your family. Could that be one of the reasons some preacher's families don't turn out so well? Maybe they see husband and dad give everyone his time and attention, except them. It's a tough balance, but it can be done. Let me rephrase—it must be done!

You can argue that Noah wasn't successful because he saved only his family. I wonder how many preachers go to sleep at night wishing for that same lack of success. Don't let your family become a casualty on the road to saving everyone else. They need "trust-building" too.

Five Final Facts about Trust

1. *You can only control one person, but that one person must be controlled.* Trust building begins with trust. And trust must be earned. And once earned and violated, it takes a long time to regain. For example, think about a treasurer that embezzles the church's money. Even if he repents and repays the debt, I doubt seriously he should be given that responsibility again. Such a decision represents wisdom on several fronts, even to the point of protecting him from future temptation and/or accusations. It is the same for preachers. There are life-positions of absolute trust that cannot be violated (physicians, teachers, attorneys, etc.) without very serious and long-

term consequences. Look into the mirror and determine that above all else, you will exercise self-control in all things. There is no trust without it.

2. *It's okay to say, "I don't know."* I was on 50,000-watt clear channel WLAC in Nashville one night with Ken Green. Brother Green fielded a question regarding an issue of importance to the caller. My brother then turned to me for commentary on the query. There was one slight problem—I had no idea what the issue was about. I said, "Ken, I have never heard of this before and therefore have absolutely no opinion on it whatsoever …" I wish I could have captured his expression on film. There is nothing quite like announcing your ignorance across the landscape of twenty-eight states! The unflappable Green grinned, thanked me for my honesty, and then proceeded to announce that he didn't have a clue either. Here it is: people aren't looking for know-it-alls on everything. In fact, they will appreciate the shortcomings of your humanity if and when you admit your ignorance. They will love you for it.

3. *Be vulnerable.* As an emotional kind of guy, it's easy for me to be touched. For example, when someone responds to the invitation in tears, well, that will usually make two of us. I have learned through the years that it's okay to cry with hurting people. Tears create an emotional bond that communicates a heart of compassion. Come to think of it, didn't Jesus sit down and cry with people, too?

4. *Shape your preaching to the moment.* You can take this to extremes, but there are times when you need to scrap what you have prepared and re-prepare. On the Sunday after 9-11, I preached about the lessons we can learn from such a life-changing event. It was not the time to talk about the sin of homosexuality or forsaking the assemblies. After a California preacher and his followers spent millions last year predicting the end of the world on May 21st, the Sunday sermon on May 22nd was not a hard one to choose. People

connect with you when you speak to the moment. It sends a message that you are real.

5. *Make deposits in order to make withdrawals.* As a gospel preacher, you will need to make withdrawals. Each time you "reprove" or "rebuke" you will make a withdrawal. People accept correction only from those that have made deposits (i.e., earned their trust). Only because they know you have their best interest at heart, will they be inclined to hear. Each time you take time for them—visiting at the hospital, crying with them at a funeral home, listening to their hurts, etc., you make deposits. Build up enough deposits and you can make effective withdrawals.

Preaching the gospel can be very disillusioning and discouraging, or it can be the most rewarding and fulfilling work you will ever do. And be advised, the devil will do everything he can to keep you focused on the former. Fight through those times and keep your eyes on the only One who can give you the incentive to endure. Preaching is not a job with a time clock. It is a work of honor, privilege, and above all, a sacred trust.

Dear Young Preacher
From Dee Bowman

"First, start with the Bible. Second, don't forget the people.
Third, be who you are. I guess that about sums it up."

This little epistle I write will be more practical than theoretical. There are several books on homiletics that are very valuable to young preachers. You might want to read *Common Sense Preaching*. It will help in that regard. For the present I want to present some timely encouragements and admonitions I hope will help you. I am not an expert, but I would like to help.

To begin, you should know that preaching is not an occupation. It's a way of living life. It's not like any other line of work in which you might engage. Actually, I believe you have chosen the highest commitment that can occupy a man's life. You have the grand privilege of preaching the gospel, of recommending the Risen Savior to a lost world, and of motivating the people of God to a higher, more dedicated service in His kingdom. But again, please be advised that you have also decided upon a profession that will not only captivate, but dominate your life. It will bring you great joy at times, and at times, great consternation. In the contemplation of the former, the latter should not be forgotten.

Are you sure you want to give your life to preaching? Listen to some of the qualifications. You must be willing to behave yourself (1 Timothy 3:14-15), and be willing to preach the truth (1 Timothy 4:6, 11; 2 Timothy. 1:13). You must be an example of what you preach (1 Timothy 4:12; Titus 2:7). You have to be prepared to flee, follow, and fight (1 Timothy 6:11-14). You will have to overcome fear or timidity (2 Timothy 1:6-8). You must be willing to keep on when things are hard (2 Timothy 2:1-12). You'll have to give diligence to be approved (2 Timothy 2:15), and be willing to concentrate on the higher things (2 Timothy 2:22-26). You will need to be willing to suffer for the cause (2 Timothy 3:1-12). You will have to attend to the small stuff (Titus 2:15), be willing to make sharp rebukes when the occasion calls for it (Titus 1:13). You'll have to be careful to speak things that befit sound doctrine (Titus 2:1). Your emphases and concentrations will have to be on the things that have greater meaning than the mundane (1 Timothy 4:7; 2 Timothy 2:16; Titus 2:10-11).

I will now proceed to the practical. These are not hard fast rules, but in most instances, suggestions about how to do your work more effectively. They are things I have learned—some of them the hard way—which I believe can benefit a preacher just beginning this new life of work and service.

Aside from your constant contact with the Scriptures and your daily Bible study, I believe the first thing most young preachers need is to learn *the value of time management.* It is imperative that you take control of your time, that you make good use of it in the service of the Lord. Now that's not as simple as it might seem. You are a talented person or you would not be drawn to the pulpit. You likely can get up three or four points on Saturday afternoon, leaving you loose to play golf, surf Facebook, or engage in some other activity. But if you want to be a good servant of the Lord, you have to learn to manage yourself and your time. Make yourself a schedule, and then be diligent about maintaining it. Make a time commitment. Make each day count for something.

And don't get caught up in the maelstrom of procrastination. It's so very easy to decide that what needs to be done can be done tomorrow. Plan the day, and then work to make the plan work today. Don't put it off—that makes for both shallow preparation and scant attention. Priorities are important to time management. Arrange your time so that the important things receive your primary attention. But do the little things, too. Form good habits and you'll likely get it done today. Sure, there will be interruptions at times, but you still have to get done what you can today.

Read the Bible more than you read things about the Bible. It's fine to get help from outside sources, but there's no substitute for reading the Bible. A good preacher will have an intimate familiarity with the Scriptures. Daily Bible reading should be part of the habitude of every preacher—be he young or old. There is so much to be gained from it. There is much new that you didn't "get" the first time you read, so much more there than you first thought. There is joy in refreshing what you already know, and pleasure in getting a new perspective on an old passage of Scripture. There is great satisfaction in having a constant contact with God's word.

Also, prayer has to be a vital part of a preacher's life. You just need an abiding contact with God. I pray three prayers that are very short, but God has heard them literally hundreds of times: "God, help me," "Thank you, Lord," and "I'm sorry, Lord." I will sometimes pray them several times a day. I hope He doesn't get tired of hearing them. And it may seem too obvious to need stating, but I have found that I can become so busy, so preoccupied with the minutiae of my daily activities that I sometimes forget to pray. That's a shame. Prayer is a necessity for everyone, but it is a special necessity methinks for the good gospel preacher. The closer you get to God the more you look like Him.

Make friends with your dictionary. Words are the tools of your trade. Come to terms with the audience before you make your case. When you misuse or misplace words, someone in the audience is distracted by it, or it doesn't communicate. Besides, when you use a word improperly, you lose the accuracy of your statement. If I had to have only two books at my disposal, it would be my Bible and a good dictionary, preferably The Oxford English Dictionary. The new computer versions of modern dictionaries are so accessible and so easy to use that we are without excuse. Good words make good sentences; good sentences make good paragraphs; good paragraphs make good sermons. Few things are more attractive or more effective than a thing well said.

Preaching is the gospel in personality. Be who you are; don't try to be who you're not. You can't do it anyhow. You're you—and that's it. And there's a certain hypocrisy, a certain mask-wearing, about trying to be someone you're not. You're special. God has given you a special personality. Like your fingerprints or your voice graphics, they're yours and nobody else's. Use your own personality to His glory. Certainly, you should freely take from others such attributes and qualities as are useful for the development of your own pulpit demeanor, but don't be guilty of merely copying someone else's style or personality. Make it yours or don't take it. Yours is the one God gave you. Make yours better all the time, and use it to His glory.

Preaching that does not storm the will is not good preaching. Preaching is intended to be both instructional and motivational. Preaching without motivation is teaching, not preaching.

Remember, all preaching is teaching, but not all teaching is preaching. Preaching is information laced with stimulation and encouragement, with rebuke and cultivation. Preaching is intended not only to inform people, but to make them want to do better. Preach to the people, even when it hurts—even if it hurts both you and them. Your effectivity is measured by how you make the people better, whatever legitimate scriptural means it takes to do so. Strong churches are not built on weak preaching.

That means you must preach to the needs of the people. You're not there to show how much you know about the original languages, spiral hermeneutics, or some complicated Bible subject, or to expound on some difficult passage, though discussions of these sorts may be necessary at times. You're there to preach what people need. They want to hear about what they need to do, where they need to go, what they need to avoid.

They need you to meet those needs.

Let me say a word or two about "positive" and "negative" preaching.
I once heard someone say that 2 Timothy 4:3, "Preach the word, be
ready in season, out of season, reprove, rebuke, exhort," means that all
preaching should be two-thirds negative and one third positive. But
passages, such as 1 Thessalonians 2, tell how Paul and the others "...were
gentle among you, even as a nurse cherisheth her children.""As you know
how we exhorted, comforted, and charged every one of you, as a father
does his children." Does that mean we should preach things that are
two-thirds positive and one-third negative? Both affirmations are foolish.
Preaching cannot be reduced to some ecclesiastical formula; it never was
intended to be such. Preaching is intended to make people get better,
whichever it takes. When the need calls for negative preaching, preach
negative things, but when encouragement is more necessary, preach
encouraging things. Preach what the people need. In both instances, do it
in love.

Congregations are much like people—they have personalities.
*It's up to you to ascertain what is the very best way to appeal to the
personality of the audience you address every week.* Stop and give some
serious thought as to how you can best reach out to the personality of
the congregation where you are working. If you are to meet the needs
of the people, you have to know what the people are like. If you are
working in an agricultural community, learn about farming. If you preach
near a government installation, learn some of the language common to
engineers or accountants. If you preach near a university, learn about
education. Study the people—what they're saying, where they're going,
what interests them. Even the terminology you use needs to match
somewhat the personality of the congregation. No matter where you
live, learn the personality of the people. It will find its way into your
preaching; and it will make it more effective. Be interested and you'll be
interesting.

Learn to read audiences. It's not easy to keep the attention of an audience for a length of time. Consider the size of the audience to whom you're preaching. Find a way to take charge without being offensive. Take care that your terminology fits with their understanding. Interpret the signs. Learn to realize when you've "lost" the audience, and find ways to re-gain their attention. For one thing, learn the value of a well-placed pause. More often than not, it will re-establish lost contact. Watch the little people; they will ofttimes tell you by their actions whether or not the audience is in tune with what you're saying. Watch the eyes of the people. Eye contact and communication go hand in hand. Pay attention to the audience. Without their attention you have no communication.

Make effective use of your sermon time. It is foolish to keep preaching when no one is listening. People today are used to quick listening. We live in an age where a 30 second commercial can tell a complete story. That doesn't mean you should be short just for the sake of being short, but it does mean that an efficient use of your time will help get your message across. Some sermons require more time. That means you have to give special attention to making sure you can hold the audience for the duration of the message. Some sermons are better short. That means you should make sure they are not only succinct, but still effective. Too short—no time for learning. Too long—a lost audience.

Be careful about the use of special accessories such as PowerPoint. Make sure you control it, that it doesn't control you. When the audience is more bedazzled with the looks of your slides or mesmerized by the constant movement of the figures on the screen, you can lose their attention to the spiritual matters under consideration. There are certain sermons, certain types of material that benefit from the media-type presentations. But there are also sermons that are better done without such aids. It's up to you to determine what is the best way to transport your message to the people. Furthermore, media presentations are more acceptable for certain personalities than for others. You should take care and determine when and how you should use the screen media. Be careful, too, that you don't spend so much time getting your media presentation ready that you don't have very much time left to develop the material you intend to present. And remember when you use it that sometimes too much emphasis can end up being no emphasis at all.

Be prepared for controversy. Preaching the truth will sometimes bring dispute, disagreement, contention. The Scriptures affirm it and experience substantiates it. But be careful not to major in it. It can be exciting, even addictive. When controversy comes because of something you have preached, face it head-on, but be careful not to become so immersed in it that you can think of or preach nothing else. Over-involvement in controversy saps valuable energy and robs enthusiasm. Be especially careful, too, not to become too involved in brotherhood politics. It seldom produces much good. Certainly, it is proper to know about and study brotherhood issues, but be very careful about becoming embroiled in them. They can take up your time and keep you from your primary duties in the local congregation.

Learn to keep your mouth shut. That may sound a bit brutal, even boorish—especially when it's said to a preacher. But it's intended to get your attention. People are going to tell you things you didn't want to know, very personal and private things. You must maintain their trust and keep those things confidential. You have to learn to be an honest and honorable repository. Wives need to exercise extra caution regarding these matters also. And another thing—you would be wise not to get caught up in the constant activities of the brotherhood grapevine. It's often gossipy and will pre-occupy your time if you allow it. Besides, most of it doesn't concern you anyway. It's neat to be discreet.

Make friends with some older preachers. They can help you. They have years of experience that can help you avoid difficulties and pitfalls. Don't be afraid to ask about situations and conditions. Most of the time they've been there, and they can help you know what to do, even guide you through rough waters sometimes. And ofttimes it's just good to sit and talk about how things have been with them. A good conversation with an older and wiser preacher is one of the joys of being a preacher yourself.

Preachers are being constantly interrupted. There's always someone needing your time and attention, or someone who comes by "just to talk." Get used to it, brother. Actually, there is a real sense in which you belong to the people. They will want your help regarding some matter— sometimes a seeming inconsequential one—but they have a notion you can help. It's not pleasant to be constantly interrupted, but that's how it's going to be, so you may as well learn to tolerate it. And while their interruptions may come at very less than convenient times, please remember that they have a certain confidence in you or they wouldn't come to you. So instead of seeing it as an inconvenience, view it rather as an opportunity. ***Be accessible—even if it's bothersome.***

Don't be afraid to say, "I don't know." I've known several young preachers who got into trouble simply because they tried to answer something they didn't know anything much about. I was one of them. It's never out of order just to say, "I don't know." After all, you can try and find out later; then maybe you'll have a better answer. Integrity is always and forever in order.

Pride is a constant consideration for a gospel preacher. Arrogant or over-confident conduct in a preacher is very distasteful. It can cause you to elevate yourself above the people, causing you to "talk down" to the audience. You can become so inebriated with pride that your main course in preaching is to have heaped upon you the constant praise of the brethren. You will receive accolades. Receive them, but with care. The pulpit puts you in a position of strength. Temper that strength with meekness and humility. In the ultimate reality, preachers are no different than anybody else. We're all merely forgiven sinners, unprofitable servants. Keep that in mind and there won't be a tendency to become arrogant. *The only thing worse than an arrogant person is an arrogant preacher.* There is no place in a preacher's life for excessive pride.

Please be advised that the worth of a gospel preacher is not measured by how many meetings he conducts or how many lectureships he participates in. Different people have different talents, different talents fit in different places. God made it that way. Every talent is important if used in the service of God. Some of the best preachers I know are speaking on Sundays at some strip center and working at some other job during the week. There are no "big" preachers or "little" preachers in the Lord's kingdom—just preachers.

Dress is important. Whether you like it or not, sloppy dress implies something to those with whom you come in contact. Preachers represent a high cause. They should dress accordingly. Not gaudy, not showy, but in a way that says they are careful. Different personalities dress in different ways; and that's good. There certainly is no "approved" attire, but care should be taken, no matter what kind of personality you have, or where you live.

I don't have all the answers. I just want to help a little. Now, let me see if I can sum all this up for you. First, start with the Bible. Second, don't forget the people. Third, be who you are. I guess that about sums it up.

God bless you as you begin this most exciting, difficult, but rewarding journey.

How to Teach an Adult Bible Class
By Warren E. Berkley

Now the Spirit expressly says that in later times some will depart from the faith by devoting themselves to deceitful spirits and teachings of demons, through the insincerity of liars whose consciences are seared, who forbid marriage and require abstinence from foods that God created to be received with thanksgiving by those who believe and know the truth. For everything created by God is good, and nothing is to be rejected if it is received with thanksgiving, for it is made holy by the word of God and prayer.

If you put these things before the brothers, you will be a good servant of Christ Jesus, being trained in the words of the faith and of the good doctrine that you have followed. Have nothing to do with irreverent, silly myths. Rather train yourself for godliness; for while bodily training is of some value, godliness is of value in every way, as it holds promise for the present life and also for the life to come. The saying is trustworthy and deserving of full acceptance. For to this end we toil and strive, because we have our hope set on the living God, who is the Savior of all people, especially of those who believe.

Command and teach these things. (1 Timothy 4:1-11 ESV)

Your personal choice to be an evangelist is a choice to be a teacher, not just a preacher. This work will likely be done in a variety of settings: across a kitchen table, typing on a keyboard, talking on a phone, sitting in a restaurant, speaking on the radio or standing before a class of adults.

For most local preachers, at least twice a week, you'll occupy this place standing before a group of adults with an open Bible. It is a sobering situation that demands "being trained in the words of the faith," carefully avoiding what is "irreverent" and "silly" (1 Timothy 4:6-7). You must be trained in godliness yourself, and present that way of life with such clarity and challenge that people with good and honest hearts will learn and respond to set their hope on the living God. Paul said, "teach these things" (1 Timothy 4:11).

Purpose: What Is This Really About?

The purpose of teaching an adult Bible class is to expedite focus on the text of Scripture with such clarity and simplicity that the students learn God's Word, know how it should be applied, remember it, and use that truth in their daily lives. As a teacher of an adult Bible class, you cannot control the students' receptivity or response. But you must be personally clear about your purpose and let every step of your preparation be well connected to the purpose: to expedite focus on the text of Scripture with such clarity and simplicity that the students learn God's word, know how it should be applied, remember it, and use that truth in their daily lives.

Focus on the text. Even if you are doing a topical Bible study, there should be one primary text. Read that text very early, the first few minutes of the class. Ideally, the students have read this passage before the class. If you have several passages for study, try to select one that will be primary. You should read this when the class opens. Also, in your wrap-up, read that passage again as the class ends. Don't let this text become a mere departure point—a passage you read to introduce your speech about what you want to talk about. Stick to that passage, talk about what it meant in historical context, and take that discussion toward the meaning for us today. Throughout the class, your task is to keep the focus on that text or texts. Any discussion that arises or is generated by your questions to the class ought to be limited to the text or subject at hand. Focus on the text.

Learning God's word. Speaking ideally, the students are not in your class to learn statistics, stand-alone word definitions, illustrations, trivia, what's on the minds of other students, brotherhood gossip, etc. They are in this class to learn God's word. Focus on the text with such faithfulness and intensity, your students learn God's word.

Memory & Application. After each Bible class, students ought to be holding two valuable possessions: (1) a memory of the truth taught from God's Word; and (2) personal intentions to apply that truth in daily life.

Preparation: How Does The Teacher Prepare?

There are four possibilities. *(1) The teacher is unprepared.* He looks over a few verses on Saturday night while watching a TV program or checking *Facebook* (Bible study in the background). Or, he just assumes it will all come to him somehow and he will get through it or fake it. That is unworthy, shameful, and irreverent.

(2) The teacher is ill-prepared. He reads and learns what commentators have written about the text, so he has some idea what it is about. But there is no plan, little thought of well-chosen words and process, and almost no thought to connecting the text to real life. You can do better and must. (Teachers generally do not do their best work when preparing in a rush.)

(3) It is possible to be over-prepared (which turns out to be almost the same as ill-prepared). When the teacher brings into the class the definition of every word, a detailed description of every literary device in the text, a lecture about genre, a discussion of every other passage that relates in some way to the study, and 12 quotations from commentaries—it is way too much; like a stew that is loaded with so many ingredients the consumer cannot taste anything.

(4) The desired objective is to be well-prepared. You know the passage well, having read it many times in quiet, prayerful study. You are familiar with the context; you know what the words mean (though you don't need to bring every single definition into the presentation). You have a well laid out plan. You have considered and edited the time frame, allowing for productive input and you have built personal application and challenge into your plan. How do we get here?

Everyone who teaches an adult Bible class must craft their own systematic process. Your process doesn't need to duplicate or imitate any other teacher's process. You may adapt, change and revise your process as you gain experience and your faith matures. But there must be some process you follow, some orderly system that leads to a good Bible class.

The Process: Finding A Good Method For You

This is a brief look at the process I use. Depending on the passage and occasion, I may not do this rigidly, but this is the underlying approach I have in mind (though occasionally adapted):

(1) I make an effort to not depend on previously prepared material. Preachers accumulate tons of material (now especially in digital form). There is a temptation—let's say, when teaching a class on Romans 12:1-2—to simply dig into your files (paper or digital), pull up what you've done before, look it over and go with it. Usually, that's not a good idea. It can become a bad habit. Preaching and teaching "re-runs" is like eating yesterday's toast—stale and crummy. Start fresh. While you may not arrive at any different conclusions, there is a freshness you will bring to the class. Copy and paste can stifle new discoveries and kill interests. Open your Bible and get started. "You do not have to know exactly where your study will lead in order to get started. The right conclusions will emerge during the process of gathering data," (Wilhoit, Ryken, p. 160). Don't let Google do this for you. You do it. Just you and the Book is the best starting place, accompanied by prayer.

(2) Be certain you know the book you are teaching from. Who wrote Romans, under what circumstances, to what people, and for what purpose? Experienced Bible teachers may not need to review this all the time. But this is background information you need to keep in mind and which may be directly related to specific passages. Context helps you understand the textual landscape. Additionally, background and context may bear directly on answering participant questions.

(3) Read the passage from several translations. We have access (in either physical or digital form) to many good translations. Even private or paraphrased versions can lead us to some useful thoughts about a passage. The more you read the passage from a variety of translations, the more familiar you can become with the main idea and the subordinate points.

(4) Lock into the main idea, and be certain you stress that in your study and presentation. Examples—

 + Romans 12:1-2, *Living a Transformed Life*
 + James 2:14-26, *Faith Discovers Its' Existence in the Activity of Obedience*
 + Isaiah 40:27-31, *God's Perfect Strength Is Our Hope, Our Energy and Life*

Most Bible students do not come to class wanting to leave with 12 word definitions, historical, academic background, debate notes, or illustrations. They want to know what that passage means for them in their thought-life and conduct. What is it about? How should I respond? The teacher must dig for this and get his hands on this during his preparation time.

(5) Give attention in your personal study to every component of the text. Notice words, phrases, sequence, connections, mood, etc. This is the hard work of "behind the scenes" study that will likely not all show up in your class presentation. Use your resources, dictionaries, concordances, and commentaries to engage in a systematic study of the text. (Observe elsewhere in this book, there are extensive digital resources to aid you in your knowledge base. See chapters by Dan Petty, Jeff Wilson and Max Dawson).

(6) Slim it down. As you put this material into your final notes and build order into your presentation, boil it down to the time frame you have, mark out places for class input, and cut out all the fat. The notes you take into class should (a) help you move through the text, (b) enable

you to punctuate the main idea, (c) mark places in the presentation where class participants can be called on, consulted or can answer leading questions, and (d) prepare a brief well written "wrap-up" you can use the last five minutes of the class time.

(7) *Build into your final notes motivation, challenge, and emphasis on practical meaning.* Your goal is not to merely occupy 40 minutes or cover 4 more verses. Your goal is not to prove how familiar you are with "the Greek," or how much insight and interests you have in literary forms. Your goal is for people, at the end of the class, to be involved in self-evaluation and personal resolution to use God's word in their lives. Drive everything in the class toward clear personal application. Do this for the people and for the Lord.

(8) *Prepare and use a good wrap-up.* Watch the clock. If you don't get through all your prepared notes, that is all right. Be sure you take the last five minutes to wrap up. (I have a post it note or card with my wrap-up notes. I pull this out five minutes before the class ends.) A class wrap-up is like a conclusion to a sermon; it challenges people to respond, reminds them of the key points, and presses any warnings given in the text. The worst way to end a Bible class is the typical: "Well, I see by the clock on the wall our time is over. So we'll continue with verse 11 next time." As you prepare, think of one question, one point, one challenge or warning you can use to give your students a powerful wrap-up. Don't just stop.

I should stress that my process is not so fixed that I rigidly follow it before every Bible class. Depending upon the subject or location of the Bible study, I may vary my process. The point of relating this is to encourage you to develop your own process, and the earlier the better.

People: Meet Your Students

Some adult learners are self-directed and mostly self-taught. In every local church there are adults who have a rich background of consistent Bible reading, study, and research, and their knowledge base may be broader and deeper than the adult Bible class teacher. Your class work for this person will be mostly a review, but also a necessary challenge for greater application and activity, using what they have learned in life.

Some adult learners have a large reservoir of experience, but without much application of Bible knowledge. These people—when speaking up in a Bible class—will likely not be focused on the text, but rather on their experience, a debate they had, a church they left, or something they recently heard about. This kind of participant input can have some value, but must be kept in good perspective. The teacher may respond after such comments, "That's really interesting, and perhaps many of us will someday have that kind of experience. In dealing with that sort of thing, it will help us to remember what we are studying today in this important passage. ..." Get back to the text or topic promptly.

Some adult learners are silent receivers. The fact that someone doesn't have anything to say, no comments or questions, does not mean that no learning is taking place. It is an obvious social reality that there are adults who prefer to say little in a group or class setting, yet they are listening, learning, and could be some of the best students in adult Bible classes. Never imply that your silent students are not participating or not learning. In some people, there is a lively invisible participation.

Some adults in our Bible classes, sadly, are just putting in time waiting for the "real worship" to begin. Your hope as a teacher should always be that the word of God will penetrate the hard, dry soil and the interests will begin and continue. If they are coming to the Bible classes, consider that an opportunity to gradually reach and teach them. You might be surprised what is happening deep within these people, though in very small increments. Your work must be done "with all longsuffering and teaching" (2 Timothy 4:2).

Some adults want knowledge they can immediately apply. That's good. To want to make personal application is good. Do consider, however, the Bible student should not just jump to application without a good knowledge base (see Dan Petty's chapter).

Persuasion: Back To Our Purpose

Remember why you are teaching: to expedite focus on the text of Scripture with such clarity and simplicity that the students learn God's word, know how it should be applied, remember it, and use that truth in their daily lives. You must (not artificially or over-dramatically, but genuinely) convey to the students the seriousness, the passion, the sheer awesomeness of who God is, what Christ did, and how well the Holy Spirit has conveyed to us the good responses to the gospel! Some passages you will teach are stern, vivid, and dark in their depiction of sin (Romans 1:18-32). The mood or tenor of such texts must be conveyed, not only by your well-chosen words, but by your tone of voice, gestures, and demeanor (with periodic pauses such as one would use in preaching, to let the students ponder the matter and re-focus their attention). Other passages you will teach are more about the blessings, the joy, and the beauty of holiness and heaven (Romans 8:18-39; Philippians; 1 Corinthians 15). The effective Bible teacher will not "act" the same way in presenting these texts. He must speak with delight and joy and uplift the people with the promises of God, challenging them to think on these things and respond. (See also brother Earnhart's chapter and reference to passion.)

Precaution: Managing Class Discussion

The format you follow in teaching adult Bible classes will depend on several conditions: your personal presentation style, the "personality" of the group, the wisdom of the elders, and the arrangement of the location (large auditorium, small class room setting). My thinking is that one cannot dictate the dimension of participation from the discussion versus lecture style, or some combination. If class participation is a part of what you do, you hold the key to how that is handled. You may find it necessary to make it clear that a Bible class is not an open forum for people (unprepared with respect to the text or subject) to hijack the class and just say anything. Participants with some agenda can literally ruin a

Bible class and turn it into something far away from the purpose. Watch for that and speak with your elders and experienced teachers about how this can be managed. There can be very valuable input from students if they stay on task, exercise brevity, and avoid monopolizing the class. My personal preference is to follow a format I'm comfortable with and my students appreciate: (1) Welcome the class to the occasion; (2) pray; (3) read the text; (4) remind us of the context; (5) offer an exposition of the text —with stopping places for leading questions or comments; and then (6) wrap up with practical challenge. Other teachers, with great results, may start out asking leading questions and then take the class to the text. Or, beginning with review questions from the previous class may be best for you. You don't have to figure all this out before noon tomorrow. But you must pray and learn from others and devote yourself to doing better. (See Charles Willis' book, *Effectively Teaching Adult Bible Class*, for valuable help in managing class discussion and crafting good questions).

Remember, young preacher, in addition to the obvious aim of helping people learn God's word and doing it, there is the goal of developing your students as learners. "Your teaching time is to be a stimulus, not a substitute. And the only way you'll get people personally excited about the word of God is to motivate them to get in touch with this reality firsthand," (Howard Hendricks, p.117). You are a learner teaching people to be learners.

"For to this end we toil and strive, because we have our hope set on the living God, who is the Savior of all people, especially of those who believe. Command and teach these things."

Works Consulted

1. Allen, Ronald J. and Bartholomew, Gilbert L. *Preaching Verse by Verse*. Westminster John Knox Press.
2. Brackett, Charlie. *Bible Study for Joy and Profit*. Clarion Word Publishing, 2008.

3. Garlock, John. *Keys to Better Preaching*. Faith Library Publications.

4. Hendricks, Dr. Howard. *Teaching to Change Lives*. Multnomah Publishers, 1987.

5. Kercheville, Berry. *Preparing the Young Man to Preach*. Harwell/Lewis Publishing Co., 2004.

6. Smith, John A. *Teaching: The Heart of the Matter*. Truth in Life Adult Workbook. Guardian of Truth Foundation, 1992.

7. Wilhoit, Jim and Ryken, Leland. *Effective Bible Teaching*. Baker Book House, 1988.

8. Willis, Charles. *Effective Bible Teaching*. Guardian of Truth.

9. Zinsser, William. *On Writing Well*. Collins, 2006.

Dear Young Preacher
From Frank Jamerson

There is nothing wrong with thinking for yourself,
but there is something wrong with supposing
that you are the only one who can think!

Teaching the gospel is the greatest work on earth, because it produces the greatest results—the salvation of souls. In addition, you get to associate with the best people on earth, eat at the tables of some of the best cooks, and then you get paid for all your work! However, like when we get married, problems can be avoided if someone tells us what to expect and gives us guidelines before we get into it.

Many young men today are having the opportunity to work for a period of time with an older preacher, and this is very beneficial, but many do not enjoy that benefit. Most of us older fellows did not have that opportunity, and as a result have made some mistakes that could have been avoided. It has been my privilege to have had a number of young men to work with me, and we have learned from one another. Older preachers are just men who happen to have been here longer. You need not be intimidated by working with older preachers. They are on your side. They are your greatest supporters and are happy to see you progress. Regardless of whether you have that experience, hopefully these letters will help you in some of the "nuts and bolts" of the wonderful world of preaching.

Preaching Is a Lifestyle

First, I would suggest that every young man understand that preaching is not a forty hours a week job. It goes far beyond preparing sermons and teaching classes at the building. In fact, as one young man who worked with me said, "It is a lifestyle, not a time clock." Certainly, you need to spend time in the office preparing sermons and Bible classes, by studying the word of God and good books that have been written by Bible scholars. If you will spend at least four hours in the office five days a week, studying God's word, you will not run out of subjects to preach. None of this Saturday night rush to search the Internet for a sermon for the next day! So, if you begin to run dry on what to preach, look at the time you are spending in study, and get back in the Book! There will be times you will want to spend more time studying some subjects, but you should plan time in the afternoons for visiting, home studies, etc. In my opinion, anyone who thinks preaching is an eight-to-five job in an office needs to find a different work.

You will need to take time for your family, especially your wife. If you are not married, you had better marry a lady who is committed to Christ and willing to live in the proverbial fish bowl. Your wife will either make you or break you. Also, you need to take time for your children. Too many preachers, while trying to save other people, lose their own children. I must confess that when I was young, I was so busy teaching home studies that I did not devote enough time to my children. In fact, the elders of one of the congregations told me to take a night off for my family. They should not have had to tell me that. Frank Andrews once said, "If you are sincerely trying to do right, when your children grow up, they will forget the mistakes you made." That has brought me comfort.

Personal Evangelism

Every young preacher ought to develop, or use a previously written series of lessons for home Bible studies. If we stand in the pulpit and preach that people should "seek the lost," and we stay in the building and wait for other members to bring someone to the building so we can preach to them, we need to listen to our own lessons. If you do not want someone else to do your work of preaching, then don't expect them to do your personal work.

There is a preacher story (one that is not true, but illustrates a truth) about a man who drove by a church building and saw a long line of people waiting to get into the building. Curiosity caused him to turn around, park his car, and get in line to see what was attracting such a group of people. When he got inside the building, he saw Jesus chained to the pulpit. He asked why He was chained there, and with tears streaming down His cheeks, Jesus said, "This is what My people have done to Me. Anyone who wants to hear My message must come into this building."

There are many good ideas about how to do personal evangelism, and it is fine to study them, but none of them will work unless you ask, "Will you study the Bible with me?" It is usually better to study with one person, or family, at a time in their home. The reasons are: (1) if you have several people in a class, some of them are good prospects and some are not, and those who are not can poison the atmosphere for those who are, and (2) it is much easier for a person to call, or simply not show up, if they have to go to your home. At least that has been my experience.

There is nothing that builds enthusiasm and promotes spiritual growth in a local church more than seeing people baptized into Christ. When they see you doing it, they are much more likely to be motivated to practice the same. Remember too, that those who are baptized need to be taught. Too many of us have baptized people and then left them to fend for themselves spiritually. While they are still excited about being new Christians, be sure to teach them the things they need to know to grow in the faith.

Also, remember to protect your reputation. Never go into a house with a woman alone to teach the Bible. If there is not going to be anyone else there, take someone with you. You do not have to be guilty of wrong to be accused, and even if an accusation is false, it will destroy your influence.

Be Careful About New Truth

One thing that causes many young preachers problems is that they learn some new truth and get into the pulpit with it before they have presented it to an older preacher who has probably heard that idea before. That does not mean that you should not study and search for yourself, but if it is new, there is probably a good reason. It was my good fortune to know good men like Franklin T. Puckett, Clinton Hamilton, and others who would take the time to answer questions for me. On one occasion, another young preacher, living in the same city with me, heard a new doctrine from a brother who had more opinions than Carter had liver pills. We discussed the issue and could not answer his argument, so he preached it from the pulpit and caused a lot of trouble. I decided to write brother Puckett and present the argument to him. He soon wrote back and tore the argument to shreds. It was new to me, but it was not true. ***There is nothing wrong with thinking for yourself, but there is something wrong with supposing that you are the only one who can think!*** I realize this is supposed to be a letter and not a sermon, but if you need a biblical example of this principle, think about the problems caused by Rehoboam's refusal to listen to the advice of the older men. He divided God's people and needlessly caused great harm in Israel. Many church divisions could have been avoided if preachers had sought and followed advice from other faithful men who had been through similar problems.

You Are A Preacher, Not A Policeman

Many young preachers think that they should preach on a subject until everyone agrees with them. A preacher who became a good friend of mine, Bob Crawley, came to Richmond, Virginia, where I began my full time preaching. He was asked to speak, and I will never forget his lesson. He spoke on the work of a preacher. The first time he said, "A preacher is a preacher, not a policeman," I thought, "Surely he is not talking to me." Later, he said, "A preacher's work is to teach the law, not to enforce it." If I remember correctly, he made the same point a third way. I distinctly remember thinking, "He must be preaching this to himself, because I'm the only other preacher here!" Really, *a great burden is removed from your shoulders when you realize that you are not accountable for making people believe, or live right.* Your job is to preach, not to police. God does not hold us accountable to learn, or live for others. He expects us to teach what the Bible says and to apply it in our own lives. The hearers are responsible for what they believe and practice—not you!

Benefit From Criticism

Because of our public role, we may receive criticism that is unjust. There is a difference between defending the truth and defending our manner of presentation. In my early years, an elder came to me saying that some members had come to him saying they thought I was angry because of emphasizing some points pretty forcefully. So in the pulpit the next week, I apologized for leaving that impression. Afterward, some members came out the door and said, "If I had to preach to this bunch, I would be angry all the time!" Several said they didn't feel that I was angry. The elder who had come to me was standing nearby listening to the comments and said, "One of those who praised your preaching was one who had done the criticizing!" Someone once said, "If your feathers get ruffled, oil them so criticism will slide off." You will be criticized at some point—all of us are. But realize that often when brethren do not want to apply the message, they attack the messenger. You can still benefit from the criticism. When some brethren give you a hard time, let your life be your defense; set up another home study and keep on doing the work of an evangelist. That's the best therapy you can receive!

Avoid The Gossip Trap

One other thing that can break confidence and cause untold trouble is getting into the gossip trap. If something is told to you in confidence, and many things will be, that means DO NOT REPEAT. Even if it was not told in confidence, some things do not need to be broadcast. All it takes to cause a big blow up in a congregation is for the preacher to begin telling things that would have been better kept silent. Generally we discuss things with our wives, but there are times when even they do not need to hear some tasty morsel that was entrusted to us.

Conclusion

Because of my failing health, an important lesson has been impressed upon my mind. When we arrived recently for outpatient medical services, a gentleman from another congregation was in the waiting room. Assuming that he had come for treatment, we began talking, and discovered that he had not come for his own benefit. Years ago, while in a gospel meeting there, the local preacher and I had visited his wife in the hospital. That visit was almost twenty years ago, and he had come to wait with me just because of that kindness! That impressed on my mind how important small deeds can be. If a man can remember such things, surely our God is cognizant of our small deeds.

It has been my observation that many congregations take on the character of the preacher and his family. If you want the congregation to be friendly, hospitable, and loving, exemplify those things (and make sure you thank your wife for most of it).

I appreciate the opportunity to share these thoughts with you, and hope that they will be helpful in your pursuit to learn, live, and teach the wonderful gospel of Christ.

How to Use and Not Misuse the Biblical Languages

By Jeff Wilson

We've all seen it before (and some of us have done it ourselves!): the preacher ascends to the pulpit and proceeds to preach on some topic or text. Today let's say it's Luke 4:4—"Man shall not live on bread alone." And so the preacher heads to the Greek: "Thayer's defines "'live' / *zao* as 'live, be alive, etc.'" and "Vine's gives the following definitions for *zao*: "'live, remain alive, etc.,'" all accompanied by packed PowerPoint slides detailing the various potential meanings of the word. And at the end of this recitation of meanings and definitions for the verb *zao*, we are left with the profound insight that "*zao* in this passage means 'live'"—just like all the English translations said.

That's an extreme example, to be sure. But it makes the point well enough: preachers—particularly younger ones—have been known to try to strengthen their sermons by an appeal to the original languages (typically limited to Greek and the New Testament, though occasionally some will tread into Hebrew and the Old Testament) with less than impressive results.

In and of itself, our interest in the original languages of the Bible is a fine and noble thing. Given the supreme authority of the text of Scripture that we rightly recognize, the basic motivation to handle that text as precisely as possible is good and right. Good intentions, however, do not necessarily produce the best practices nor do they prevent misuse, even of the unintentional sort.

There are a number of reasons for why we misuse the original biblical languages. Sometimes it is just a matter of making honest mistakes.

Perhaps we've never thought much about it before, never thought about how language works as it conveys meaning between people. Maybe we are just following the examples of others we have heard and admire. Sometimes we think we are adding substance to our sermons, making them more accurate or thorough, or perhaps demonstrating to our brethren that we worked hard on our material. And sometimes, if we are honest enough to admit our flaws and vulnerabilities, we may choose to invoke the biblical languages because we want to have a certain authority or credibility over our brethren who are listening to us. *For some, the "appeal to the Greek" is considered a silver bullet, something that ends the argument. If we are not careful, we can give in to the temptation to try to force our listeners into submission by making fancy arguments for which they have no way to test the validity of themselves.* And young preachers especially are living in a phase of their preaching work in which they desperately want their listeners (virtually all of whom are older than them, more life-experienced than them, in many cases wiser and even more knowledgeable about many things—biblical or otherwise than them) to take them seriously. When we are young we yearn for credibility and the temptation to try using the biblical languages to make our preaching and teaching more credible (at least in our own minds) sets us up for problems.[1]

A crucial part of the problem in why biblical languages tend to get abused is that many of us only know one language: English. People who know at least a second language—ancient or modern (Spanish, French, etc.)—are well aware of the hazards and challenges of accurately moving thoughts expressed in one language into another. Additionally, in learning another language we become much more aware of how language in general works, as well as how different English (and thus our assumptions about language and communication) can be from many other languages, including the biblical ones.

Furthermore, the typical way that we appeal to the original languages is almost always to do word studies so as to define words. We turn to *Thayer's* or *Vine's* for help with Greek words the same way that we turn to *Webster's* to help with English words: to get a list of possible meanings. We are searching for some exegetical insight we assume can be found in some nuance of a word's definition in the original language (and occasionally this actually is the case!). Yet much of the time, the definitions of the Greek words rarely vary in any significant, meaningful way from their English translations. ***Knowing the range of possible meanings for a word does not in fact help us to decide what a word in a particular instance actually does mean.*** A number of other factors aside from dictionary definitions—such as context for instance—come into play when deciding what a specific word means in a specific usage. Real insights through biblical languages don't become more common until we move beyond dictionaries and into the realm of syntax and grammar, and, even more so, into the realm of literary sensitivity (word plays through assonance, repeated key terms that indicate emphasis, subtle chiasms based on word gender, case endings, or word order, etc.). The fact of the matter is that when it comes to what the original languages can actually do for our understanding of the biblical text, word-study-as-definition is actually one of the lowest levels on the stairway of meaning.1 Two examples will serve to demonstrate the point.

Understanding The Limits Of Word Studies

Here is the translation of Jeremiah 1:11-12 from the New American Standard – Updated Version: "The word of the LORD came to me saying, 'What do you see, Jeremiah?' and I said, 'I see a rod of an almond tree.' Then the LORD said to me, 'You have seen well, for I am watching over my word to perform it.'" On a first reading, this seems to be an odd oracle: what does Jeremiah's seeing a rod from an almond tree have to do with God watching over His word to perform it? A trip to *Vine's* to look up definitions won't really help us here. We will just discover that the Hebrew words are well translated by the English words given. Yet Hebrew does hold the key to getting the point here, but a word-study as we typically do them will not find it. This passage makes its point through a clever wordplay in Hebrew. In Hebrew, the word for "almond tree" (*shaqed*) and the word for "watching" (*shoqed*) sound alike. This oracle depends not upon the meaning of the words as much as upon the *sound* of the words. Jeremiah's seeing a piece of a *shaqed* ("almond tree") is a way of punning into the fact of God's determination to *shoqed* ("watch over") His word—that is, to see it certainly accomplished. The pun is the key part of the meaning of the text, but just looking at Hebrew definitions in *Vine's* or another lexicon will not actually get you to the real persuasive power of this oracle.

Now, take a more substantial example from the New Testament—the conversation between the risen Christ and Peter in John 21. Here we have the reconciliation scene between Jesus and Peter: Peter is given three opportunities to confess his love for Christ in a way that parallels his three-fold denial of Jesus on the night of His betrayal. The sermon that many of us (myself, admittedly, included) have preached over the years from this text focuses on the alternative uses of the Greek verbs for "love," where Jesus keeps inviting Peter to profess his *agapao* love for Him, while Peter is only willing to confess a *phileo* love for Jesus. Finally, on the third exchange, Jesus switches to Peter's word and simply asks Peter if he loves him in the *phileo* way. Our sermons here focus on the different "definitions," where the verb *agapao* is supposedly defined as being a higher, self-sacrificial love, while *phileo* is merely the love found in friendships. Thus the exegetical point we try to make out of this passage often has to do with the quality of love that Peter is struggling to offer to Christ. And here our word-study definition approach to using Greek has failed us.

D.A. Carson, in his commentary on John, gives a very thorough response to this understanding of these two Greek words for love—and in so doing reminds us about the need for caution in depending solely on the word study approach for attempting to interpret the original language text.[2] First, a long-term perspective on the use of *agapao* in Greek literature suggests that it was becoming the standard Greek word for "love" in general, which is why the NT uses it as the preferred term for love. Secondly, the Septuagint (LXX) usage of *agapao* and *phileo* shows that these two words for "love" could be used interchangeably with no obvious difference in nuance or significance (cf. Genesis 37:3-4 for instance). Finally, in the larger context of his gospel, John has already demonstrated that he uses these two words for love interchangeably as well. The Father "loves" the Son in John's gospel, and in 3:35 the verb *agapao* is used, while in 5:20 the verb *phileo* is used. Elsewhere Jesus is said to "love" Lazarus and in 11:5 *agapao* is used, while in 11:36 *phileo* is used. Similarly, the uniquely Johannine designation "the disciple whom Jesus loved" can use either Greek word—*phileo* in 20:2 or *agapao* in 19:26. The words for "love" used in John 21 are varied most likely for stylistic reasons—the same reason we do not use the same words over and over again in paragraphs that we write, but instead use synonyms to break up the verbal monotony. Indeed, in John 21, Carson notes that "[i]n addition to the two words for 'love,' John resorts to three other pairs: *bosko* and *poimaino* ('feed' and 'take care of' sheep), *arnia* and probate ('lambs' and 'sheep'), and *oida* and *ginosko* (both rendered 'you know' in v. 17). These have not stirred homiletical imaginations; it is difficult to see why the first pair should."[3] And so, such an example serves to remind us about how much more goes into using the original languages correctly than just looking a word's definition up in a source that may or may not be accurate.

So, How Can You Use Biblical Languages Rightly And Well?

How, then, can we use—and not abuse—original languages in our teaching and preaching? I want to make a couple of general observations that will hopefully set the stage for how younger preachers (and anyone, really) can be better in handling Greek and Hebrew in their studying, preaching, and teaching. But because of the relatively small space of this essay versus the large topic of tools and techniques for handing Greek and Hebrew, I want even more so to make some recommendations for further reading.

First, become a better reader and writer in English and that will invariably improve your sensitivity to biblical language. For many of us, English was not our favorite subject in school and we have never fully, thoroughly understood our own native language as to how it works and conveys meaning. Our English vocabularies are not as robust as they could be. We do not tend to spend much time thinking about how context, literary devices like metaphor, word plays, stylistic variation, or irony work in our own literature. By becoming a better student of your own language you will naturally become better able to understand how to get beyond the word-study-as-definition approach to exegeting biblical passages.

Second, if you really want to avail yourself of the insights that the original languages can give, your best recourse is quality commentaries written by scholars who are truly competent to address linguistic matters. I naturally hesitate to give this advice since such commentaries virtually always are written from perspectives with which I disagree to varying extents. There is potential danger on this point. But the reality is, given the aforementioned role of grammar and syntax, context, historical patterns of usages, and literary devices in affecting the meaning of individual words in the original languages more so than their dictionary definitions, if you cannot read these languages for yourself, then you are simply going to have to depend on guidance from someone else who can if you want to mine these linguistic insights. Think about it this way: if you were given a copy of Dostoevsky's *The Brothers Karamazov* in the original Russian along with a copy of a Russian dictionary, how confident would you be that you could accurately handle that novel's meaning simply by looking up the definitions of individual Russian words in the text? Yet we essentially try to handle the biblical text this way with the methods that we sometimes use.

As for resources, the good news is that there are a number of books that are available and relatively inexpensive and that are intended to give people with little or no knowledge of the original languages guidance in gaining some benefit from those languages. Some of these books also give their own good explanations of better reference works (lexicons, grammars, etc.) that will better serve those who want to well use these ancient languages than the relatively outdated and occasionally inaccurate Vine's and Thayers'.

At the head of the list is William D. Mounce's *Greek for the Rest of Us*. The subtitle says it all: "using Greek tools without mastering Greek." The thing that makes Mounce the right person to write this book is that he is the author of one of the more effective and useful beginning Greek grammar books of the past couple of decades; it is widely used, student-friendly, well laid out. Furthermore, Mounce has substantial experience both teaching Greek to students in an academic setting as well as teaching those outside of academia who are not learning the language yet still want to avail themselves of some of the basic reference works that Greek-readers use.

Another important book that even those who *do* know Greek (and/or Hebrew) ought to read and be familiar with is D. A. Carson's *Exegetical Fallacies* (2nd edition). This volume reads like a source book of common Bible study errors (some of which you can unintentionally commit without even trying to use original languages!) that will be eye-opening. If nothing else, read Carson's powerful first chapter on "Word-Study Fallacies"; it will do you much good!

One newer reference tool worth noting as useful to preachers young and old is Mounce's *Complete Expository Dictionary of Old & New Testament Words*, produced by the above mentioned William D. Mounce.

It is very similar to Vine's, but more up-to-date and accurate with regards to its material. As an added bonus, the volume has a brief essay at the front that gives an abbreviated methodology for doing original language word studies and thus not misusing the reference work he has produced.

There are a few other books worth briefly mentioning for those who are interested in exploring Greek further. David Alan Black, *Using New Testament Greek in Ministry*, is useful, though its intended audience is those who have at least some limited proficiency in Greek. The chief value of this book for readers of this essay would likely be Black's chapter on the different Greek tools, resources, and reference works that are available (though Black is a bit dated now in this regard). For those who want to explore more closely how biblical words convey meaning, Moises Silva, *Biblical Words and Their Meaning: An Introduction to Lexical Semantics* is challenging but helpful, especially chapters 3-6.

For those who want to try their hand at Hebrew, the companion volume to the first Mounce book is Lee M. Fields, *Hebrew for the Rest of Us.* This work seeks to give a very basic overview of how Hebrew works and how to use the various reference works available for that language. Paul D. Wegner, *Using Old Testament Hebrew in Preaching* is a small, very recent volume that has an extremely useful chapter detailing the various study tools available for Hebrew. That chapter also has an up-to-date section on various computer software options for Bible study (information equally useful for those principally interested in Greek).[4]

The Bottom Line

You can know the truth without knowing or using Greek or Hebrew. You can be an effective preacher of the gospel without appealing to the biblical languages. You can bring glory to God and serve the kingdom well without making things more complicated than they have to be. The essential message of God's revealed will to humanity is clear in any major, responsible translation, and we need never lose sight of that simple reality.

If, however, you want to use the biblical languages, this essay is not intended to discourage you so much as it is to sober you. The essential message of God's word is clear enough, but the original languages can beautifully add color, nuance, and precision to our understanding of and delight in God's word. Yet it takes effort to reap those benefits: a more intentional and accurate understanding of how language works, a recognition of the limits of word studies in elucidating the riches of the original language text, and a dedication to doing the reading and studying it takes to mine the biblical text in its original form, as opposed to a quick cut-and-paste definition dump from Vine's into a sermon document. This takes much more time and effort than most have typically realized to do it rightly and well. It is certainly not for everyone, and that is quite alright. But in an age where so many people want to be proficient at various things without putting in the long-term effort to properly acquire that proficiency (everybody wants to be an all-star, nobody wants to practice!), you need to recognize that real, honest skill with the original languages of the Bible will be no different. There are no shortcuts, only dedicated effort. Earn the ability to use biblical languages accurately and appropriately if you can. But even more so, the real challenge for young preachers is to become comfortable with your own unique talents and abilities and don't try to be something you are not. That's certainly true for using original languages as well. The Lord will make us adequate for the work He wants each of us to do.

End Notes

1. Cf. David Alan Black, *Using New Testament Greek in Ministry* (Grand Rapids: Baker, 1993), 75: "Although lexical analysis [i.e., word studies, JTW] is important, it is a limited tool, a servant rather than a sovereign. As a professor of Greek, I have never worried much about my students' ability to do word studies; I am always far more anxious that they will stop there. Too much New Testament preaching tends to be 'word bound' and to ignore the broader context in which words

are found." Black goes on to note the work James Barr in emphasizing that meaning is principally conveyed by sentences (i.e., words in relationship with each other) rather than individual words with isolated definitions.

2. What follows is drawn from D. A. Carson, *The Gospel According to John* (Pillar New Testament Commentary; Grand Rapids: Eerdmans, 1991), 676ff. For a similar conclusion cf. Andrew T. Lincoln, *The Gospel According to Saint John* (Black's New Testament Commentary; Peabody, MA: Hendrickson, 2005), 517-518.

3. Carson, John, 677. Carson adds this observation: "Amongst those who insist a distinction between the two verbs is to be maintained in each verse, there is no agreement. Thus, Trench insists *agapao* is philanthropic and altruistic, but without emotional attachment, and therefore much too cold for Peter's affection. That is why the apostle prefers *phileo*. By contrast, for Westcott *agapao* denotes the higher love that will in time come to be known as the distinctively Christian love, while Peter cannot bring himself to profess more than 'the feeling of natural love,' *phileo*. Bruce wisely comments: 'When two such distinguished Greek scholars (both, moreover, tending to argue from the standards of classical Greek) see the significance of the synonyms so differently, we may wonder if we are intended to see such distinct significance.'"

4. Bible study software can be a wonderful tool to expand access to research tools and make Bible study faster, but computer use still does not change the basic issues addressed in this essay. Consider the advice regarding computer Bible software by Andrew H. Wakefield, "A Word About…Bible Study Software," Review & Expositor104.1 (2007): 22 – Software "can put too much power into inexperienced hands. Someone using this software may be tempted to use Greek and Hebrew, for example, without actually knowing enough about either language to interpret the results responsibly.

Likewise, someone without enough background to judge the relative values of the different resources included in a software package may be tempted to use results indiscriminately. In short, this kind of software can give someone the illusion of more knowledge that he or she actually has, and thus can lead to authoritative-sounding pronouncements that are not actually well informed."

Dear Young Preacher
From Paul Earnhart

"… the things that you have heard from me among many witnesses,
commit these to faithful men who will be able to teach others also.
You therefore must endure hardships as a good soldier of Jesus Christ"
2 Timothy 2:2-3

Ever since Paul took young Timothy as an apprentice from Lystra and Barnabas took John Mark to Cyprus, a biblical pattern has been set for older and more experienced gospel preachers to nurture and mentor young men into becoming capable evangelists in their turn. Able heralds of God's word do not live forever; it is their task not only to preach as long as they themselves have breath, but also to help raise up younger evangelists to replace them. There is even an indebtedness to these younger men that rises from all the help and encouragement we ourselves received from older preachers when we were young and untried. Paul's charge to Timothy (2 Timothy 2:2) to pass on what he had learned from him to other faithful men who would be able to teach and train others also is still working its way through history. There is nothing more lacking in grace than a seasoned evangelist who has no time for young men and who seems to find them and their earnest questions a burden. The apostle Paul, though no longer living, is still training young preachers through his example and his letters, especially those to Timothy and Titus.

Young men who today are drawn by their love of lost people to the preaching of the gospel are a treasure and it is a privilege to join with other experienced preachers in offering them encouragement and counsel for their chosen labor. Preaching is a work of the greatest significance with consequences that transcend time. All of us who take it up will be compelled to recognize with the apostle Paul that we are in ourselves inadequate for the task (2 Corinthians 2:16b).

Only God can make us sufficient for such an immense undertaking (3:5). Therefore, if any fruit is born from our preaching it is to God and not ourselves that the glory belongs (1 Corinthians 3:5-6; 1 Peter 4:11). It is in His word that the power resides and even our ability to preach it comes from Him.

Nothing so much suits the character of a gospel preacher as does humility. Therefore we should handle the gospel with utmost gravity (2 Timothy 2:15) but not take ourselves too seriously. As our "beloved brother Paul" has observed, "we do not preach ourselves, but Christ Jesus as Lord, and ourselves your bondservants for Jesus' sake" (2 Corinthians 4:5).

Preaching Must Not Be a Profession

How we view preaching is very significant with all kinds of implications. Let me warn young aspirant preachers against viewing preaching as a profession in the same category with law, engineering, medicine, accounting, or carpentry. Those are honorable ways of making a living, but gospel preaching must never be approached merely as a means of livelihood. It is that attitude that causes preachers to go wherever the money is greatest and the circumstances most comfortable and not where the need is most urgent. Preaching can become nothing more than the function of a carnal ambition. Such men will preach as long as it enhances their portfolio, but when it ceases to do so will catch another train. The financial support provided to preachers by churches and/or individual disciples has plenty of biblical precedent (1 Corinthians 9:13,14; 11:7-9; Philippians 4:15,16). But men who will not preach save for money are unworthy of the gospel they propose to preach. Such financial fellowship is not the defining mark of an evangelist but a means by which a man is enabled to enlarge a work which he will do whether with or without it.

The preaching of the gospel ought to be a function of being a disciple of Jesus Christ, not of a job, a career, or a profession. The support provided is neither benevolence nor a barometer by which to judge the success of a career. The most critical call is not the so-called "call" to preach but the call to follow Jesus. It is this commitment to deny oneself and take up one's cross and follow Jesus (Matthew 16:24) that will produce true workers in the kingdom of heaven whether it is preaching or some other equally valuable work. Let no man serve God for money and "suppose that godliness is a way of gain" (1 Timothy 6:5). That is the spirit of the hireling who has no ultimate concern for anything or anyone other than himself and who will refuse to suffer hardship (2 Timothy 4:3,4).

Young men often ask how they are to know whether they should aspire to preach or not. My answer has always been: "You become the most devoted disciple of Jesus you can be and you will get your answer." The most remarkable thing about true preachers is not their ability to communicate God's word to others but the fact that they "have been crucified with Christ" and they no longer live but Christ lives by faith in them (Galatians 2:20). When you have given yourself away to the Lord, whatever abilities you have will be His. If you have the ability to effectively preach Christ, you will do it no matter the sacrifice or the difficulties. Not to do so is not a failure as a preacher but a failure as a disciple which is profoundly more significant.

Preaching Must Be Servant Work

No matter the popular impression, preachers are not the spiritual elite of the kingdom. Preachers are just Christians trying to serve the Lord according to the "measure of faith" which God has given them (Romans 12:3-8; 1 Peter 4:10,11). When they prove themselves good stewards of those abilities ("gifts"), they have done no more than any other child of God who has served and honored the Lord with what was given to him. Those who spend their lives in preaching Christ should be loved and regarded for their work's sake, but no more so than any other faithful disciple, man or woman. A great disservice is done to the cause of Christ when preachers are turned into a "clergy" class, a spiritual breed apart. They are ministers of the Word but they are not "the minister" of local churches. There are many ministries (works of service) in Christ, and many "ministers" who are not preachers (Mark 10:43; Acts 12:25; Romans 12:6-8; Ephesians 4:12).

Like Paul, those of us who preach must make ourselves "a servant to all" in order to win as many as possible to the Lord (1 Corinthians 9:19-22); indeed we must become "bondservants" to them "for Jesus' sake" (2 Corinthians 4:5). And we don't do this because we are preachers, but because we are disciples of the Son of God who has set for us an awesome example (Philippians 2:5-8).

Preaching Must Be Passionate

There is nothing more unappealing than one who preaches Christ devoid of feeling or passion. Those of us who preach are dealing with the grandest and most compelling theme known to man. Surely the one who preaches the message must have been touched by its fire. Jeremiah said that God's word was in his heart "like a burning fire shut up in [his] bones" (Jeremiah 20:9). It is not a question of volume or shallow dramatics but earnestness—an earnestness that rises naturally from the heart and character of the preacher. It cannot be simulated. It is a matter of a truly good man speaking about that which he is deeply convicted. He is the Lord's disciple!

This passion, if it is to be truly Christ like, must be a passion for lost people. No man can succeed in preaching who does not love people and wish to engage with them regularly. They are clearly the object of divine concern. Jesus came into the world for no other purpose than to seek and save the lost (Luke 19:10; 1 Timothy 1:15), and the preaching of the gospel has been divinely chosen as the means to achieve it (1 Corinthians 1:21). Preaching that has any other purpose is a perversion.

When you preach, don't preach down to the audience as if you were talking at them instead of having a conversation with them. Someone has aptly defined preaching as "one side of a passionate conversation." Try to make the hearer feel that the message is for him and not at him.

Do your best to get out of the picture yourself and allow the hearer to have an encounter with God and His word. Remember that we are only messengers—clay pots entrusted to carry the precious treasure of God's word to the world (2 Corinthians 4:7). The power and the glory are in God and His word.

Preaching Must Be Christ-Centered

The call for Christ-centered and cross-centered preaching has been viewed by some as a code word for soft-pedaling all that Jesus and the apostles taught about the church and godly living. To the contrary, Christ-centered preaching will make teaching on those subjects all the more powerful. This appeal is simply to say that God's redemptive work through His Son is at the heart of the gospel and should be kept there. Paul called the gospel "the word of the cross" (1 Corinthians 1:18) and to proclaim it was to "preach Christ and Him crucified" (1:23; 2:2) and to declare the significance of the death, burial, and resurrection of Jesus (15:1-4).

This great central truth of the gospel—what God has done to save sin-ridden men from ultimate disaster—must always be the foundation of our preaching. God, not man, is the hero of the story. In the work of reconciliation, "all things are of God" (2 Corinthians 5:18); that is, the initiative for salvation and the provision of all those things necessary to it came wholly from Him. It was not, is not, and never will be a human achievement. We will never be able in the very smallest sense to glory in ourselves (1 Corinthians 1:29; Ephesians 2:8, 9). It is the will of God that the One who is "the fullness of the Godhead bodily" (Colossians 2:9), and who "made peace by the blood of His cross" (1:20) should have "the preeminence" in all things (1:18). That is the very reason that in the preaching of the gospel, God's work in saving us must always occupy the high ground, rather than what we need to do to be saved.

But this truth in no sense diminishes the importance of telling lost men and women what they must do to be saved or of teaching them to observe all that the Lord has commanded (Matthew 28:19). What we are urging is that God's great story should be surely known by the sinner before the matter of his response to it is raised. The venerable W. W. Otey warned in 1950:

> We have often made great efforts to convert people to the legalistic form of the gospel and church, lacking much of the spirit of Christ. The apostles made every effort possible to convert the sinner to Christ …

> We might cry out, 'You must repent', but that alone can never bring the sinners to repentance. The person of Christ must be presented to the mind and heart of the sinner till he believes with his whole heart. The terribleness of sin must be earnestly driven home to the heart of the sinner till he abhors and turns from his sinful ways (*Living Issues*, pp. 135-136).

In short it is the knowledge of God and what He has done in His Son that makes His word compelling. We must strive to convert sinners to Christ rather than to a system. Once converted to Christ as Lord all that He has commanded will be more readily received.

Preaching Must Be Balanced

The just quoted W. W. Otey, who was no stranger to controversy and waged a strong battle against the digressions of his day, made a very wise observation about balance in preaching. "'Preach the word; be urgent in season and out of season; reprove, rebuke, exhort.' Try to be a balanced preacher. Negative preaching must be done. But negative preaching never did build. At best it clears away the ground for building. It requires preaching the whole truth as far as possible to build the house of God"

(Ibid). Brother Otey's exhortation is well-spoken. Jeremiah was given just such a commission by the Lord, "To root up and pull down, To destroy and build, To build and to plant" (Jeremiah 1:10). There are two things we need to remember. First, that the gospel of Christ is "good news." It is a positive message. It may not begin in a comfortable way, with a clear indictment of our sins, but at last it is the most comforting thing in the world—a message of mercy and forgiveness, reconciliation and fellowship, peace and joy. Second, we must realize that in every positive there is an inherent negative, that is, anything that would frustrate God's gracious purpose for His people. Such things must be opposed and rejected.

In view of this the preacher of the gospel, though he must not always see everything in terms of issues and controversies ("to the man with a hammer everything looks like a nail"), he cannot fail to deal forthrightly with pernicious errors and ungodly behavior that would put God's people in jeopardy of losing their souls. In this he may be attacked and maligned, but he must never allow it to embitter him, but rather cause him to rejoice that he is counted worthy to suffer shame for the name of the Lord (Acts 5:41). The spirit of Christ must always prevail.

Expository preaching can be a great aid to balance in preaching. It helps one to study and to address subjects and areas of Scripture that might be otherwise neglected. Topical preaching has its value too, but when done exclusively, a preacher can find himself addressing favorite subjects, especially those that bring a positive response, and neglecting some that are needed even if not welcomed so warmly.

The Preacher Must "Take Heed to Himself …"

Paul was much given to this exhortation when dealing with those who teach and lead others. To the elders at Ephesus he entreated, "Take heed therefore unto yourselves, and to all the flock …" (Acts 20:28). To the one who would help his faltering brother he wrote, "restore such a one in a spirit of gentleness, considering yourself …" (Galatians 6:1). And to the young evangelist Timothy he appealed, "Take heed to yourself and to the doctrine" (1 Timothy 4:16).

It is a great temptation to preachers to take their preaching as a surrogate for their own spiritual growth and development. It is a well-known fact that one can issue great spiritual challenges to others without attempting to lift them with one finger (Luke 11:46). Preachers can preach without listening to or applying their preaching to themselves. This is no doubt the reason for Paul's oft-repeated exhortation for those who teach to first take a careful look within. ***It is possible for evangelists to become skilled word merchants who know how to speak effectively but make no effort to live up to their own message.*** It is a grave kind of hypocrisy. Even Paul himself with all the devotion with which his life was characterized wrote concernedly, "I discipline my body and bring it into subjection, lest when I have preached to others, I myself should become disqualified" (1 Corinthians 9:27).

This is the reason why all of us who preach the gospel need to spend serious time addressing our own spiritual growth. Paramount is time regularly spent reading the Bible devotionally and not merely in preparation to preach. And no less important is time devoted to prayer. Indeed more time ought to be spent praying than preaching. We cannot succeed in doing God's work without God's help. We cannot speak effectively of that which we ourselves are not experiencing. Paul's exhortation to his young charge Timothy in 1 Timothy 4:12 speaks principally to character and not to rhetorical skills: "Let no one despise your youth, but be an example to the believers in word, in conduct, in love, in faith, in purity." A facile tongue does not a preacher make. So, young brothers, nothing is more important to your success in preaching the gospel of God's Son than the earnestness of your own devotion to the One whose word you proclaim.

Those of us who have gone before you will be praying that you will preach God's grace even more effectively than we have. We will be your most supportive listeners, ready to help and encourage any time you need us. So preach the Word with all that is in you, and trust God for the rest.

The Preaching Calendar
By Mark Roberts

Consider these two different scenarios. It is Saturday night in brother Willy Nilly's office. Once again, Willy is struggling. He loves to preach, but he hates writing sermons. Most of the time the week somehow seems to get by him, and he finds himself in his study on Saturday night trying to bang out a lesson. An idea comes to him, but it really needs more work to develop. He looks at a random passage in his Bible, but he thinks he may have spoken on something similar only a few weeks ago. What will he preach in only a few hours? Saturday nights are agony, and that means that for the brethren where Will preaches many Sunday mornings aren't real good either. Frankly, some are concerned because brother Nilly seems to preach poorly organized lessons that often are mostly concerned with whatever was recently on the news. There is also a disturbing rumor that a fair amount of brother Nilly's outlines aren't his but instead come off the Internet.

It is also Saturday night at brother Plan's home. He isn't in his office working. Brother Plan rarely works Saturday evenings, choosing instead to spend time with his family or entertain members of the congregation. Having Saturday nights "off" doesn't seem to affect his preaching, however. His sermons are always fresh, timely, and varied. He often announces well in advance what he is preaching on, and can tell the song leader what to prepare for. He preaches series and often, even if not in a series, the Sunday morning lesson and Sunday night lesson go perfectly together. *There is a sense of cohesiveness to the pulpit.* **It seems to have direction and purpose.** Mostly what the brethren worry about at the congregation brother Plan preaches is if some other church is going to try and "steal" their preacher. They love him and look forward to his preaching.

What's the difference? Some people will say brother Plan is a better speaker than brother Nilly, but that's not true. If preaching were nothing but an oratorical competition, brother Nilly would win the blue ribbon. The difference is in planning. Brother Plan plans his preaching. Brother Nilly doesn't. As a result, while one is effective in his work, enjoys preaching, and finds satisfaction and fulfillment in it, the other preacher often contemplates getting out, and he may soon find brethren helping him to do so.

While there might be some debate as to the importance of the sermon in all that a preacher must do (Is it more important than evangelism? Good Bible class teaching?), there can be no doubt that most congregations expect to hear well-crafted and well-delivered sermons on Sunday. That makes preaching a vital and important work that ought to be carefully planned. This chapter will challenge you, the local preacher, to consider a regular, well thought out plan for your preaching.

Before we get to the mechanics of creating a preaching plan, let's take a moment to examine what the Bible says about planning. Sometimes planning gets a bad rap as people talk about "going on faith" or misunderstand what James is teaching about planning (see James 4:13-16). The truth is God honors planning throughout Scripture. Moses is shown a model so that the construction of the tabernacle, God's very home, can be properly built (Exodus 24-40). David understood a similar giant organizing effort for the temple (see 1 Chronicles 22-29). Nehemiah carefully planned the wall rebuilding he superintended (Nehemiah 2-3). Paul planned his preaching trips (see Romans 15:24, 28; 1 Corinthians 16:5-6). Jesus even planned (note Luke 9:53). God even plans: "this Jesus, delivered up according to the definite plan and foreknowledge of God, you crucified and killed by the hands of lawless men" (Acts 2:23) [emphasis added]. Planning simply recognizes that time is a limited resource and determines to be a shepherd of what God has given us (see Ephesians 5:16).

If you are not planning what you are preaching, then you are missing out on the benefits that come with a definitive, written out, long range plan for your preaching. Those benefits include *making preaching easier.* No more anxiety Monday to Saturday as you wonder what you will preach. No more late Saturday nights frantically working on what you finally decided to "go with." Further, planning means *you don't repeat yourself.* When we have a plan we can see where we have been and carefully make certain that we do not accidentally go there again. Planning will also help you *command respect in the pulpit.* We want people to take our preaching seriously. Many of your members have to plan and schedule their work and activities. When they see that you take preaching seriously enough to have a preaching plan they will appreciate that and value you and your work all the more. Finally, planning allows you to preach series. Series preaching can be effective, but it needs to be planned carefully to miss spring break or the start of the deer hunting season!

How then does one go about putting together a preaching plan? Let me offer some suggestions based on how I develop my preaching calendar. This is not intended to be definitive, or the end-all on this subject. Others do things differently, and I encourage you to listen to what others say, take the good, and adapt your own style for planning. How you plan is up to you. What should not be optional is planning!

First, develop a monthly lesson plan. In a typical month most preachers have eight preaching "slots." You have four mornings and four evenings. What do your people need to hear across a month? In Acts 20:27 Paul tells the brethren at Ephesus he preached "the whole counsel of God" in his three-year work there. Am I doing that in my local work? Probably not if I am just scraping up something off the Internet on Saturday night. Without a plan I will end up preaching on what is easy to work up, or whatever I am currently interested in. Instead of preaching what is easy or interesting to me, I need to be thinking about what the church needs. How much first principle preaching do I want to do? What about something for young people? What about preaching expositorily through a book of the Bible? Sit down with a sheet of paper and put eight lines on it. Mark them "Morning" and "Evening" to represent the eight sermons preached each month. Then decide what to put in each slot. I try to preach a first principles sermon every first Sunday of the month. I also preach through a book of the Bible, usually on the third Sunday night of the month. I try to preach explicitly on Jesus, His teaching or actions, once a month. We use a preaching theme for the year—something the elders have asked me to emphasize twelve times over the course of the year. I usually preach that sermon on the third Sunday morning of the month. Carefully I put these goals for my preaching on my monthly schedule. I should add here that prayer is an obvious must as we go through this process.

Then I print out a three-month calendar so I can see the twenty-four Sundays I will preach that quarter. I remove meeting dates and take notice of any special occasions like Easter or Mother's Day when we will have extra visitors. Then I take those monthly goals and write them on to the calendar. On this Sunday I will preach on Christ. This Sunday night will be the expository lesson. The calendar now has the general ideas for the quarter's sermons all filled in, and I am ready for step two.

Second, use your HOT IDEAS folder to fill in the specifics of the quarterly plan. Most preachers have a folder they drop all sorts of stuff into that might make a sermon someday. In the folder are notes they took on a chapter of a book they read, something they saw on the Internet, a good article from a brotherhood periodical, or an idea that came to them as they were doing their daily Bible reading—it all goes into that folder. This is the holding tank where sermons go to simmer (and sometimes die!). I get my Hot Ideas folder out and start going through it. Any Jesus sermons in here? Anything on the preaching theme for the year? I begin to sort through it all, putting sermons in their proper place on the calendar. Of course, when you first start this process your Hot Ideas folder may not yield enough sermons, requiring you to come up with some sermons "from scratch" to fit the categories you have decided needed to be preached. That is okay. However, the longer you use this system the more sensitive you will be to what needs to be dropped into the Hot Ideas folder. When a quarter ends and you grab the Hot Ideas folder to start planning the next quarter you will be surprised how many good ideas and sermon starters are waiting for you to put them on the calendar!

Third, keep dropping material into the Hot Ideas *folder to support that quarter's sermons.* If you know you are preaching on pornography and see a good article on that topic, then clip it out and drop it in the folder. If you see an illustration for that upcoming sermon on worship then in the folder it goes. You will be amazed at how much you find that goes perfectly with the preaching you have planned to do, because now you are aware of what you will be presenting. Your ears will "perk up" when those topics come across the news, your web browser, or in your reading and studying. All of that supporting material goes into the folder.

Fourth, write that sermon! When you are ready to construct this week's sermon, get out your Hot Ideas folder and see what you are preaching on this week. Also check and see what material is in the folder for that sermon. Pull it all out and begin working! You are now writing a sermon that you planned and prayed about, have been thinking about and germinating or stewing on for some time, and that has all sorts of helpful material ready to launch that writing effort. You will find that sermon writing time will fall dramatically while your sermon quality may rise significantly. Best of all, the congregation won't have to sit through any more "Saturday night specials!"

Some may ask how "set in stone" my sermon plan is. The answer is that I try very hard to preach exactly what I planned to preach, but there will be some exceptions from time to time. One Wednesday the elders came to me to tell me that a situation with a member had reached a crisis point, and they would have to withdraw from her on Sunday. They wanted me to preach a sermon on church discipline that morning to prepare the congregation for what was about to happen. They got the sermon on discipline they requested. Other events may make a change necessary. The Sunday after 9-11 many preachers felt that their people needed a word from God in that terrible crisis and scrapped what they had planned to speak on. All of that is fine. The sermon plan isn't revealed from God nor is it Gospel! It is something we come up with to help our work. We can modify it as we see fit. Of course, sometimes what you planned to preach on and thought (during planning) was a tremendous sermon idea simply doesn't "gel." You thought it would make a sermon, you tried to make it into a sermon but … it's just not getting there. So a change will have to be made for that week. That is okay and it happens. But generally speaking you will find that it is easier to stick to your schedule than to vary from it.

As an added benefit, your calendar will help you in two more key areas. First, it will insulate you from someone who is sure you were "shooting at him" because he happened to attend that morning. When you explain your calendar and that the sermon brother Belligerent heard was actually scheduled several months ago the steam gets taken out of irate brethren in a hurry! That leads directly to the second benefit—you will appreciate God's providence even more. It is incredible how what I write down three months in advance somehow seems to be just the right thing that the congregation needs for that Sunday. People will sometimes jokingly ask if I have been living with them because the sermon was so on target that day. This only builds more trust in me that if I will make myself available to the Lord, He will see to it that what is written in those blanks on my calendar will be what needs to be put there!

I hope brother Willy Nilly decides to change his ways before he (or his family or the brethren) get fed up with preaching and he gives up. What he needs is a little self-discipline that will lead to carefully planning what he will preach. Peter says, "Therefore, ***preparing your minds for action,*** and being sober-minded, set your hope fully on the grace that will be brought to you at the revelation of Jesus Christ" (1 Peter 1:13) [emphases added]. Wise preachers will prepare their minds for action by planning their preaching!

How to Make Your Delivery More Effective
By Don Truex

O ur world is radically different than that of our first century counterparts. We work jobs they would not understand, travel in ways they could not imagine, and communicate with technology beyond their dreams. We dress differently, speak a different language, and entertain ourselves differently. But the one constant in our churches from the first century to the twenty-first century is the primacy given to the preaching of the gospel

The importance of that task is not simply the biased observation of one who has given his life to that work but, rather, an affirmation of biblical truth. In his majestic prose, Paul blended three elements of the single theme of reconciliation with God, namely, the "ministry of reconciliation," the "word of reconciliation," and the "ambassador" who pleads for men to "be reconciled to God" (2 Corinthians 5:18ff). The primary application of that text clearly has reference to apostolic ministry. But there is, without question, an application to be made to twenty-first century preachers as well.

In the ancient world, an "ambassador" represented the interests and authority of the king or emperor in a foreign land. It is much the same today. Spiritually, "our citizenship is in heaven" and yet on this earth we represent the interests, uphold the name, and speak on behalf of the King of Kings and Lord of Lords. By any measure, that is a formidable task.

For most of us, spending 30 to 45 minutes twice a week with each individual member of our congregation is an impossibility. But we do have the opportunity to speak with each of them for that time period via our presentation of the gospel. Through our preparation and presentation, we have the opportunity to help earthly Christians apply eternal principles.

But let's be honest—genuine communication is a challenge. Connecting with an audience whose attention span has been diminished by the media and whose learning patterns are often more visual than oral will demand our very best efforts.

See Yourself Clearly. The beginning point of preparation and presentation is not opening a Bible in one's office or stepping into the pulpit of a congregation. It is, rather, the formation of a person who is worthy to be heard. That formation is the result of a determined effort to be the man God calls us to be and of a concerted effort to have relationships of honor with those we serve.

It was Donald Miller in his work Fire in Thy Mouth who correctly observed, "The Bible is the supreme instrument in the cultivation of the minister's own soul. Behind every sermon there must be a man, and the primary function of the Bible for the minister is to produce that man. The Bible is not for the minister chiefly a quarry of texts; it is rather the starting point from which he grows a soul. And if he is not in the process of growing a soul, his ministry is spiritually doomed before he begins."

Quite simply, the most valuable thing we can do to enhance our presentation of the gospel is to "grow a soul" that allows us to speak from a life of integrity.

Evaluate the World Honestly. The late John R.W. Stott was correct when he noted in his classic work Between Two Worlds that the preacher finds himself with one foot in the biblical world and one foot in the modern world. Our task is to build a bridge between those worlds that is paved with the word of God.

Jesus did this in a masterful way via the parables. He used stories of borrowers and lenders (Luke 7), suffering and Samaritans (Luke 10), friendship and prayer (Luke 11), bigger barns and barren souls (Luke

12), loving dads and rebellious sons (Luke 15). Each story contained an element of daily life along with a nugget of eternal truth. I have often told young preachers that every sermon should ultimately answer the "So what?" question. Why does this teaching matter? What difference will this make in my daily life that will lead me to eternal life? It was Harry Emerson Fosdick who observed, "Only the preacher proceeds still upon the idea that folk come to church desperately anxious to discover what happened to the Jebusites." Good information? Indeed. But how does that biblical truth translate into the life of the Christian who must live in a culture that is often antagonistic to his faith? That application is the task of the preacher.

No wonder Paul reminded his young protégé Timothy: "All Scripture is inspired by God and is profitable for teaching, for rebuking, for correcting, for training in righteousness, so that the man of God may be complete, equipped for every good work" (2 Timothy 3:16,17).

Communicate God's Word Effectively. Effective presentation occurs only when the focal point is divinity not humanity. Listen to Paul: "My speech and my preaching were not with persuasive words of human wisdom, but in demonstration of the Spirit and of power, that your faith should not be in the wisdom of men but in the power of God" (1 Corinthians 2:4,5).

Simply put, the pulpit is not my platform for promoting my personal preferences, conservative or liberal politics, or gaining a personal following for myself. "For we do not preach ourselves, but Christ Jesus as Lord, and ourselves your bondservants for Jesus' sake" (2 Corinthians 4:5). There is no substitute for God's word. PowerPoint is not a substitute. Illustrations and physical props are not a substitute. And there is no substitute for all of God's word. My goal is to leave this life and be able to say with Paul, "I am innocent of the blood of all men. For I have not shunned to declare to you the whole counsel of God" (Acts 20:26, 27). If it were up to me, I'd preach forever from Luke's gospel and James' epistle. Both are fast paced with practical applications leaping off the page. But though homiletically and exegetically more challenging, I am a better preacher for making the effort to mine the "whole counsel of God" contained in the totality of Scripture.

Effective communication demands that I understand something of my audience. Some will have been Christians for 60 days and others for 60 years. Some are visual learners while others are oral learners. Any given audience will be composed of different genders, different generations, different economic circumstances, and different spiritual backgrounds. Those differences create presuppositions that color their view of both Scripture and the God who gave it. Speaking effectively to such diversity will always be a challenge.

One final thought before we deal with some of the "nuts and bolts" of presentation. When the preacher of integrity has successfully built a bridge between the Bible world and the modern world through the effective communication of the gospel, it is entirely appropriate to challenge your audience to respond. I have always believed that the "invitation" is not solely for those needing to be baptized but for all of us. It is an invitation to apply what we've heard, and we should challenge the audience to do so. Read the Mountain Message and hear Jesus call for His audience to act. Listen to His preaching that commanded, "Take up your cross daily and follow Me" and "Go into all the world." God's goal was never to give us information in order to win games of "Bible Trivia" but to impart information that leads to transformation in life. Effective, Bible-based preaching should deepen faith in God, move people closer to God and motivate sacrificial service for God.

"Where the Rubber of Faith Meets the Road of Reality." I am simply a preacher, not a philologist or professor. I do have a bit of mileage on the odometer of my life, and it is from that perspective that I offer the following as practical thoughts about effective delivery.

First, Philip Brooks, who died in 1893, famously noted that preaching is "the communication of truth through personality." The truth must be God's and the personality must be yours. I tried hard in my early years to mimic my heroes of preaching. Thankfully, I failed in that endeavor. I can be no one but myself. You can be no one but yourself.

Second, be a "clean vessel" who is "useful to the Master" (2 Timothy 2:21). It is true not just about moral matters but life in general: You cannot call on your audience to discipline themselves to the Master's teaching if they see any area of your life in which you are clearly undisciplined. Your passion, eloquence, preparation, and presentation will be negated if your audience senses that you are unwilling to take for yourself the medicine you prescribe for them.

Third, there is no substitute for preparation. One of the co-editors of this volume noted years ago in his book, *Men at Work*, that "You earn the right to speak by preparing." He was correct in that observation.

I have been with my current congregation for 18 years. On my first Sunday in the pulpit, I promised the church that I would never stand before them unprepared. I believe I can say with integrity that I have kept that promise. Could I "wing it" after three and a half decades of preaching? Yes, I could. But I would know, and God would know, and eventually my brethren would know that I was giving less than my best effort. Listen to James, "My brethren, let not many of you become teachers, knowing that we shall receive a stricter judgment." As a shepherd in the congregation I serve, I will "give account" for the souls under my charge. As a preacher in the congregation I serve, I will be weighed in the balances of "judgment" for the work I do in "handling aright" the word of God. Again, there is no substitute for preparation.

Fourth, remember that "if the bugle gives an indistinct sound, who will get ready for battle?" (1 Corinthians 14:8). If your language is imprecise, your argumentation esoteric, your presentation scattered, how is your audience to be edified? How will the non-believer in the assembly "worship God and report that God is truly among you?"(1 Corinthians 14:25).

We must remember that the highly educated, intellectually gifted apostle observed, "And I, brethren, when I came to you, did not come with excellency of speech or of wisdom declaring to you the testimony of God. For I determined not to know anything among you except Jesus Christ and Him crucified…my speech and my preaching were not with persuasive words of human wisdom…" (1 Corinthians 2:1, 2, 4a).

One of my early mentors was known far and wide for his powerful presentation coupled with immanently understandable content, all delivered in a relatively short window of time. And yet, for the simplicity of his content, he was one of the best read preachers I've ever known. He possessed a voracious appetite for learning and yet was able to effectively transfer God's word from his impressive intellect to his listener's heart. We would all do well to remember that complexity does not always equal depth.

Fifth, critique your delivery. A friend came to me recently and reported that he had watched the video of his delivery of the Wednesday evening invitation in our church. He confessed that it was the most painful experience which he had voluntarily endured in his lifetime! Listening to or watching yourself preach is a singularly uncomfortable experience. And yet, it is a valuable experience. We hear inflections in our voice and nuances in our speech patterns of which we are unaware. We see gestures, movements, lack of eye contact that need to be improved upon. In short, we hear and see reality rather than the skewed perception of self-analysis.

Sixth, always understand that your passion will be contagious. Puritan theologian and preacher Richard Baxter wrote, "I'll preach as though I ne'er should preach again, and as a dying man to dying men." My father preached for 60 years. During my teenage years, he developed a voice issue that necessitated surgery. Whether he would ever preach again was known only to God. I well remember the Sunday before his surgery—the truth he taught, the love for souls he expressed and the urgency with which he approached his task. Thankfully, his voice was strong for many more years. But I've always remembered that Sunday and do my best to replicate that enthusiasm, giving both God and brethren my best when I preach.

Seventh, remember that we are preaching the gospel—the good news of a God who loves and a Savior who redeems. Yes, there is a time when we must "reprove and rebuke." And yes, there is much to be against as we encourage our auditors to "deny ungodliness and worldly desires." But we must never lose sight of the fact that the "[good news] of Christ" is "the power of God unto salvation" (Romans 1:16). We must never lose sight of the fact that "God desires all men to be saved and to come to the knowledge of truth" (1 Timothy 2:4). The privilege of preaching that message, the task of touching souls for eternity is one that deserves the very best that we have to offer.

Dear Young Preacher
From Melvin Curry

Serving the Lord and other people is what preaching is all about.
Remember that God is first, others are second,
and you are third (Philippians 2:3-8).
So, do not elevate yourself.

I commend you for choosing to preach the gospel. However, the advice I offer you comes from the perspective of one who has primarily supported himself and his family through secular work. I will begin by sharing with you a few autobiographical circumstances that led to me to become an evangelist. Then, I will offer some advice that I hope will help you in your work as a preacher.

My college years began in pursuit of a degree in accounting, but I soon changed my major to chemistry. By my sophomore year, I had already determined to preach the gospel, but I also desired to teach at the college level. As I struggled to make up my mind which direction I should go, little did I realize that ultimately I would do both.

I had preached my first sermon in the spring of 1951 to two elderly women who were worshiping in the area just north of Dade City, Florida. After reading from the Scriptures, I looked up and discovered that both of them appeared to be asleep, and their appearance did not change until the end of the sermon. Immediately, they became alert and joined in singing the invitation song. When the service concluded, I was given $1.50 (half of the contribution) for travel expenses. That was an inauspicious beginning, but it launched a lifetime of preaching. The next Sunday I preached for the small congregation in Pine Castle, Florida, near my home town of Orlando. On the third Sunday, the

Temple Terrace church asked me to preach. I did and received $40 (a lot of money in those days), with which I bought a new Bible, a new suit, and MacKnight's *Commentary on the Epistles of Paul*. I can count on my fingers the number of times since then that I have not been privileged to preach at least every Lord's Day of the year.

In the spring of 1953, I married Shirley Castleberry. She has supported me in all my prayerful decisions about moving from place to place to preach or to pursue my educational aspirations. I love her for being a stay-at-home wife and mother who has been devoted to her husband and children. Her godly example has been an inspiration to the whole family. Despite all the hardships she has endured, she has never reacted negatively or complained. I truly believe that a godly marriage mimics life in the Garden of Eden. It is a haven of peace where one can be free and enjoy the fullness of the blessings that the Lord provides on this earth.

Although you may already have begun to preach and have mapped out the plans for your life, be prepared for a multitude of twists and turns. In 1954, about a year after graduation from college, I moved with my wife and our first child to Grandview, Missouri, to work "full-time" with the church there. Not too many months later, however, I obtained the group's consent to engage in part-time work for a while as a rural mail carrier in order to supplement my income in order to meet our obligations. When three years elapsed, I felt the urge to continuing my education at the graduate level, and we left Missouri in pursuit of that goal. Wherever we subsequently lived, however, I kept receiving invitations from congregations to preach and teach in their communities. Eventually we moved to Illinois, where I enrolled in a graduate program at Wheaton College.

We experienced many ups and downs in a variety of circumstances while we were in the Chicago area, but I was able both to continue my work of preaching and to complete an M.A. degree from Wheaton. At first, we lived in Oak Park, Illinois for about nine months. I was going to school, working in Department Stores, and preaching for the small group that met on Central Avenue in Chicago. Then, Leslie Diestelkamp, who preached in Berwyn, persuaded me to move with the family to Oak Lawn, Illinois, and begin work with the Burbank Manor congregation. We did so and remained there for three years. When the Diestelkamps went to Nigeria, however, we moved to Berwyn and labored with the Christians there for three additional years.

Those were six good years, and the work with both churches had gone well. In 1963, however, I had an unexpected invitation to teach at Florida College, and my wife agreed to make the move to Temple Terrace, where we continued to live for 34 years. From 1963 until the present (for 48 years), I have been able to serve some wonderful congregations that could not supply full financial support to those who taught among them. You, too, can help similar churches if you choose the route of secular employment to support your family.

One might say that my change of direction demonstrated a lack of faith. No, I believe it was a matter of personal choice. I greatly respect and honor those who have been fully supported by churches to do the work of an evangelist. But most men in the body of Christ have never been in such a position to preach and teach. Rather, they have engaged in honorable secular occupations to the glory of God, and they have devoted themselves to the service of their Master. Fortunately, today many churches have sufficient financial resources to support one or more men to preach, either at home or overseas; you may in good conscience work with one of these groups (1 Corinthians 9:9-12), praising God for the wonderful privilege. In times of great economic uncertainty, however, I would suggest that you secure training in an occupation you can fall back on if necessary.

You may grow weary and waver in your commitment to proclaim the gospel. Sources of discontent range from the indifference of brethren to doctrinal departures from the faith. I confess there were times I became discouraged and thought about quitting. But, like Jeremiah, when I said, "I will not make mention of Him, nor speak anymore in His name, ... His word was in my heart like a burning fire shut up in my bones; I was weary of holding it back, and I could not" (Jeremiah 20:9). "If I preach the gospel," Paul said, "I have nothing to boast of, for necessity is laid upon me; yes, woe is me if I do not preach the gospel! For if I do this willingly, I have a reward; but if against my will, I have been entrusted with a stewardship" (1 Corinthians 9:16-17). Thus, I have never been able with a clear conscience to escape the stewardship of preaching. And, most likely, neither will you be able to do so.

If you are firmly committed to be a "man of God" (1 Timothy 6:11; 2 Timothy 3:17), you must determine to be apostolic in your preaching and teaching. This will draw you closer to the Lord. And there is no other way to "save both yourself and those who hear you" (1 Timothy 4:16). Luke said that the first group of Christians "continued steadfastly in the apostle's doctrine" (Acts 2:42), and Paul commanded Timothy to commit the things that he had learned from him "to faithful men who will be able to teach others also" (2 Timothy 2:2). Never break this chain of responsibility. Pass on the apostolic teaching, from person to person, from house to house, both at home and abroad.

The correctives for individual and church problems are loyalty to apostolic teaching and godly living. Imitate the apostles as they imitated Christ (1 Corinthians 11:1). Follow their teaching, because Christ guided them into all truth (John 16:13). Their doctrine provides "the pattern of sound words" (2 Timothy 1:13; cf. Titus 2:1). Their words are healthy in themselves and produce health in those who accept them. They constitute divine traditions to be handed down from generation to generation (2 Thessalonians 2:15; 3:6; cf. 1 Corinthians 11:2). Thus, "Guard what was committed to your trust, avoiding the profane and

idle babblings and contradictions of what is falsely called knowledge"
(1 Timothy 6:20; cf. 1 Timothy 5:21; 2 Timothy 1:13-14).

Know the Scriptures: "book, chapter, and verse." You will never be
able to acquaint yourself with everything that is false. But if you know
what is true, you will be able to recognize what is false. The way to detect
a counterfeit $100 dollar bill is to be familiar with the genuine article.
Study it thoroughly—smell it, taste it, and analyze it in every detail.
Examine the quality of the paper, of the ink, of the engraving, of the
special marks of identity—all you can learn about it. Similarly, know the
Scriptures thoroughly.

Knowledge of the Bible is the first order of business; the craft of
sermon preparation and delivery is secondary. Homer Hailey once
gave a good answer to a young preacher who asked about the relative
importance of Bible study and sermon preparation. He responded by
relating the advice his mother gave him about milking a cow. "Homer,"
she said, "First, you must get the milk from the cow, then worry about
hitting the bucket." In other words, "Learn the word of God, then learn
the techniques of preaching." But both are important.

Be yourself and not a clone of someone else. When I first began
preaching, I would start my sermon with a typical James P. Miller
introduction, "Now in the beginning of my part of the program, I
want to say that I am glad to be here." I would conclude with one of
N.B. Hardeman's eloquent endings, encouraging others to "bask in the
sunlight of God's love throughout the ceaseless ages of eternity." At least,
I did so until I listened to myself on tape. That ended that!

You should choose a respected translation of the Bible for studying,
memorizing, and teaching. I find that brethren most commonly use both
the New King James Version and the New American Standard Bible.
Anyway, do not choose a highly interpretive version. And refrain from
making your choice on the simple basis that one or the other of the
versions is supposed to better represent the Greek texts, because most

good editions of Bible translations supply the variant readings in the margins or footnotes. In other words, choose a tried and true version that will endure for many years. Your Bible will be your lifelong companion. Therefore, constantly changing translations is counterproductive. But you would be wise in your study to compare a variety of versions.

Memorize entire books of the Bible, one passage at a time. Brother Charlie Bailey used a unique method and committed to memory the entire New Testament. He would memorize a passage, including one or more verses, and would drop a penny into a bowl. Later, if he could quote it without a mistake to someone else, he would put another penny into the bowl. If he made a mistake, however, he would take the penny out. When he had about a dozen pennies in the bowl, he would advance to the next passage. Perhaps a different method would better suit you, but the sooner you begin the process the better. Be careful, however, to observe passages in their context. Thus, you should read a book of the Bible over and over again before attempting to memorize it. The relationship between words, sentences, and paragraphs is absolutely essential to the meaning of the whole.

Read profusely and critically, carefully considering other viewpoints. Truth has nothing to fear. But filter everything through the lens of God's word, not the other way around. Build a balanced library, both printed and digital. I have been impressed that men like Alexander Campbell, Moses E. Lard, Racoon John Smith, J. W. McGarvey, Isaiah B. Gubbs, and R. L. Whiteside had a thorough knowledge of the literature of their times. Be sure, however, that you read what your spiritual ancestors had to say. New books are not always the best. Moreover, read primary source materials whenever possible, and be very skeptical of what you read in secondary sources.

Quote your sources both fairly and accurately. Love demands no less. Any given sermon, article, or conversation is a very limited expression of a person's ideas. On occasions, I have spoken or written things that were unclear, misleading, or downright false. Fortunately, most folks have been kind and have given me the benefit of the doubt, but not always. Keep in mind that you do not know another person's intention, unless he expresses it to you (1 Corinthians 2:11a). If you believe someone has seriously erred, then ask them for clarification. If you cannot do so, then think the best and not the worst. Many problems among brethren could have been averted by this simple procedure.

Think for yourself. Hopefully, you will be attuned to apostolic teaching on most matters. But this may not always be the case. All of us stray both doctrinally and morally. Also, novelty of thought should not be your goal. However, as you study the Bible, if you come up with what seems to be a fresh idea, test it over and over again before publicly teaching it. The saints do not need more new opinions; we need the truth of God. Unfortunately, I must add, truth can be very unpopular.

The ideal situation is to build a circle of close friends who will keep your disclosures confidential, but who will offer you honest, intelligent criticism (Proverbs 27:17). Some of these friends should be older brethren who have long ago heard most new things. They usually are less inclined to permit you to go beyond a tolerable limit. In other words, don't make the mistake of Rehoboam, who rejected the counsel of "the old men" in favor of the advice of "the young men" (1 Kings 12:6-11). Both he and Israel paid a terrible price for his foolish action.

Moreover, listen to the sisters, especially the older ones. As the story goes, a young man preached an unusually long sermon. Afterwards, an elderly sister requested to talk with him in private. Pulling him aside with the crook of her walking cane around his neck, she said to him, "Young man, that sermon was entirely too long." He quickly responded, "Why, Acts 20:7 says that Paul preached until midnight, and I didn't preach nearly that long." Then she replied, "There are three things you need to know about that example. First, you are not the apostle Paul. Second, if I went to sleep, fell out of the pew, and killed myself, you couldn't raise me from the dead. Third, that was the last time Paul would see those brethren, but you will be here for quite a while." Our good sisters in Christ are intelligent and have a lot of common sense!

Each person is unique, and *you* have something special to offer in your work. Genuineness, sincerity, and humility are essentials in the service of love. Serving the Lord and other people is what preaching is all about. Remember that God is first, others are second, and you are third (Philippians 2:3-8). So, do not elevate yourself. Even if others attempt to put you on a pedestal, don't let it go to your head because sooner or later you will fall. There will even be times when some folks deliberately knock you down. In either case, get back up as gracefully as possible. The more frequently people see Christ in you, the more they will respect you for who you are.

Especially, avoid being like Diotrephes. John describes him as loving his own importance and refusing to "receive" the apostles, speaking "malicious words against [them]. And not [being] content with that, he himself does not receive the brethren, and forbids those who wish to, putting them out of the church" (3 John 9-10). Certainly, there are times when brethren must be warned and withstood to the face. Moreover, within congregations, discipline is necessary when all else has failed. But God hates factious persons.

Strive for balance in your life. There will usually be enough time for study, public teaching, private teaching, visitation, a personal life, and much needed rest. But you must endeavor to keep everything in order. I have avoided using the word *schedule*, because preachers do not punch time clocks. I doubt that I would consent to work with a group that demanded such rigidness of me. A preacher must be self-motivated by a strong sense of honor as well as duty.

You will have to learn when to walk away from the pressure of your work and even from the demands that people will impose on you. Take time out to be with friends and family. Jesus slipped away from clamoring

crowds of people who would never have relinquished to him a moment
to himself. He retired to some solitary place to pray (Matthew 14:23;
Luke 6:12; John 6:15) or took time to relax with close friends (for
example, with Mary, Martha, and Lazarus, John 12:1-2).

There will be times when your parents and relatives need you. If
you have a wife and children, they especially will depend on you to
spend time with them. To fail in these family relationships makes one
worse than an unbeliever (1 Timothy 5:8). However, if you are single
and unwilling to commitment yourself to your family, then do not get
married and have children. Before you pursue the life of celibacy, read
Matthew 19:10-12 and 1 Corinthians 7:9.

Your spouse and offspring will live in a fish bowl. They will be
scrutinized by unrealistic standards of conduct. Likely, therefore, they
will be the ones who suffer the most from your pursuit of preaching.
Therefore, they must have your love and support. Many a man has spent
so much time trying to save other families that he has lost his own. Be
determined that you are not going to let this happen in your case.

"Pray without ceasing" (cf. 1 Thessalonians 5:17-18). This will keep
you close to the Lord. Get down on your knees in the morning and pray
in secret to the Lord. Praying will give you direction throughout your
whole day. The most effective men that I have known in the kingdom
of God have been men who rely on the Savior and not on themselves.
Interestingly, Paul not only counseled Timothy to devote himself to the
word (2 Timothy 1:13; 2:15; 3:14-17; 4:1-2) and to avoid false teachers
and false ways (2 Timothy 1:15; 2:16-18; 3:1-5; 4:14-15), but also to
depend on God's power, with which He freely sustains his saints in a
variety of ways (2 Timothy 1:7; 2:1; 3:15; 4:17).

Jesus told us that there are two great commandments."You shall love
the LORD your God with all your heart, with all your soul, and with all
your mind." And, "You shall love your neighbor as yourself" (Matthew
22:37, 39). In addition, Paul said,"Let no one despise your youth, but

be an example to the believers in word, in conduct, in love, in spirit, in faith, in purity" (1 Timothy 4:12). These passages encapsulate nearly everything that pertains to the personal behavior of a preacher.

The Lord and the brethren will be watching all that you say and do, and they will expect you to do what you say. Don't get up tight about their expectations. Turn the situation around. Demand of yourself that you live a saintly life and act benevolently toward others. The more you exemplify Christ in your life, the fewer problems you should have with others.

I am excited about the prospects of your future, and I hope you are, too. A preacher's life is wonderful but wearisome. If you are up to the challenge, aware of the ups and downs, and willing to deny yourself in order to serve others, then let nothing keep you from doing the work of an evangelist.

How to Use Technology Wisely
By Max Dawson

Thanks for giving me a few minutes of your time as we explore the use of technology. You have entered the work of God in a wonderful time. You have more resources and teaching tools available to you than any generation of preachers has ever known. Yet, there are dangers and pitfalls in the very resources that we use every day.

The content of my thoughts to you will involve warnings, advice, and encouragement. Please allow me to note at the outset that I am optimistic about the future of God's work because of the quality and dedication of young men who have chosen the gospel as their life's work. I believe the kingdom may be on the verge of unprecedented growth in modern times because of the devotion of young men like you. May our God richly bless you in all that you do in His cause.

Technology: A Revolution

What we are witnessing is much more than an evolution. More than ninety percent of the technology that we use today was not available at all to evangelists of bygone days.

It was only a few decades ago that all a preacher had to work with was his Bible, a concordance, and a few commentaries. He probably had a typewriter. His teaching aids were typically limited to a blackboard and maybe an overhead projector. As far as personal technology goes, a really cutting edge guy might have a battery powered wristwatch! There were no computers, Bible programs, or word processors. Previous generations had no iPads, smart phones, or data projectors. Believe it or not, before the 1990's preachers did not have cell phones! We have witnessed an explosion in technology. About twenty years ago, when computers were first coming into use by preachers, I was using an Atari

800 computer and my coworker, Tony Mauck, was using an Apple IIe. Both were clunky, big, slow, and could do almost nothing in the way of graphics. They had crude word processors built into them and yet they were a quantum leap up from typewriters. I told Tony that we were only in the computer stone age and that we would witness radical advances as technology progressed. I don't think either of us could imagine what twenty years would bring.

What will the next twenty years bring? We can only guess. Tremendous advances are already being made on speech to text software. I speak and the words appear on the computer screen. Will we have "thought to text" in the future? Only God knows what the future will bring. While technology changes, the principles for using it do not.

Powerful computer-based study aids can reduce hours of research down to minutes. That is a great positive, but there is a downside—we no longer have to search by reading the Bible text. Some of the most important truths I have learned in over forty years of preaching I have learned while searching the text for a word or phrase. I knew it was there (maybe in 1 Chronicles), but I couldn't remember where. Reading through the book for more than an hour I ran across the phrase, but on the way to discovery, I also learned important things about King David and the Ark of the Covenant. There is nothing like reading the text itself. Technology can never take the place of reading through the pages of the Bible. "Give attention to reading…" (1 Timothy 4:13).

It is argued that technology saves us lots of time, freeing us for other tasks. I agree that the potential for time saving is there, but do we really wind up doing other tasks? While we talk about time saving, we may give so much time to technology that we have little time for evangelism. Technology provides us with tools to do the work of God, but the tools are never an end in themselves. Don't get caught up in the revolution that is technology. Rather, get caught up in the revolutionary teaching of our Savior.

Technology: Cultural Challenges

Americans live on technology.

We have to face the facts of modern technology and what it means to gospel preaching. Our culture lives its life through Facebook, Twitter, texting and email. For many folks, these things are their primary source of contact and interaction with other people. It's not all bad to use those things as contact points, but it's not all good either.

Consider also the impact MTV has had on the past generation, and the impact it has had on communication across all media. We are trying to reach people who were raised on MTV where no sight or sound is allowed to last more than 2.5 seconds. Watch any commercial on TV; watch most TV shows; visuals and audio are constantly changing. It can even create sensory overload, but it is what people have become accustomed to. As a result, the attention span of Americans is measured in nanoseconds.

And then there is multitasking. It's one of those things our kids think they do incredibly well. A kid watches a YouTube video on his iPad, carries on text conversations with five people at once, updates his Facebook page, and reads a chapter for a history test tomorrow—all at the same time. And when this kid comes to worship, you have to put a hook into him that will get him to slow down for 30 minutes while you teach him something from the gospel. You have your work cut out for you!

Preaching is more challenging than ever.

In spite of all the technology at our disposal, the work of a preacher may be more difficult today than in past generations. Like it or not, in the minds of most people you are in competition with TV, movies, music, and every other medium. If a kid (and most adults today) does not like a TV show within the first two or three minutes, he will change the channel. That's why almost every action show or movie starts off with something that hooks you right from the start.

Are we not as wise as the world on this point? Do we really think we can get up in the pulpit with carelessly prepared PowerPoint slides, make a long and boring introduction to a sermon, and thereby grab the attention of the MTV generation? Jesus said, "The sons of this world are more shrewd in their generation than the sons of light" (Luke 16:8). You may protest and say that people should come to worship with an attitude that wants to learn the word of God regardless of how it is presented. That's true, and if we lived in a perfect world, it would be that way—but we don't live anywhere near perfect!

Furthermore, when people come to worship, they come with expectations. Are they wrong in thinking that things should be done well? If things are not done to high standards, many guests will never come back.

So, you have people in your assemblies who have short attention spans, who will judge you in competition with entertainers, and who have high expectations. What do you do? I will tell you first what you don't do. You don't become an entertainer. You don't present a lesson that is a compilation of five-second sound bites. And you don't give up on people who have been nurtured in this crazy environment. So, what do you do?

You have to do your work well!

When you open your mouth to speak, the sound system should fill your auditorium. I am amazed at the number of times I have seen that a P.A. system hasn't been turned on and checked before services. When technology is carelessly used, guests will go away thinking we are a bunch of klutzes! People expect better. God deserves better.

Your PowerPoint presentation should be first class. While not every preacher is a graphics designer, every preacher can do quality work. Slides should be simple, attractive, and tell a story. Anyone should be able to look at your slides and quickly get an idea of what your lesson is about. If people can't do that, something is wrong with your slides. You should not put every detail of your sermon on the slides. Some preachers put every facet in his outline on the slides. He may have twenty or more slides, but maybe no one knew what his three points were! Attractive simplicity works! Possibly a title, a reference to the main text, and the three points of the sermon is all that may be needed on the slide. Put those things on an attractive background and reveal your points one at a time and you have what you need to help people learn! Don't be careless with your work. People expect better. God deserves better.

We serve an excellent God. He deserves excellent efforts on our part. To do less than our best is an affront to God. Read David's prayer in 1 Chronicles 29:10-17. That text helps us see something of who God is and who we are. He deserves our best efforts.

Technology: It Is Not Our Message

It shouldn't be necessary to make this point, but technology presents issues that make it necessary.

Technology can be fun. Maybe we get the latest version of PowerPoint and see the cool transitions and animations, and immediately we think, "Wait till I get in the pulpit with these. People will be dazzled." If dazzle is your objective, quit preaching and get a job with a design company.

I saw one presentation where a preacher had animations coming in from every direction. Every point and sub point used a different animation. He did not make a gospel presentation; he made a demo of all the cool stuff that his new version of PowerPoint would do.

Animations and transitions must have purpose. It isn't wrong to use transitions and animations; presentations tend to look better when animations are used. Animated text draws attention to itself, and that almost always works better than just popping text up on the screen. My point is that animation should not be a distraction. It is used to call attention to your point, not to the fact that you found a new technique.

All of this says that technology is not a toy, but is a tool that we use to communicate the gospel.

Technology must never get in the way of the message. It is only an aid to help us impart the message to hearers. While Jesus did not use modern technology, He did use teaching aids. In the Sermon on the Mount (Matthew 5-7), Jesus used more than fifty illustrations and word pictures. He talked about the lilies of the field and the birds of the air. He used those objects to make a point. They were not an end in themselves, but were used as aids to teach the truth that God cares about His people. The teaching aids that Jesus used never got in the way of the message.

Our message is the gospel. Whatever technology we use must help plant the seed of God's word deep in the hearts of hearers. The power of the gospel is in the proclamation of the Person, not in PowerPoint.

Technology: Some Do's and Don'ts

Here is some practical advice on the use of all sorts of technology. Since technology goes far beyond computers, I include lots of other stuff in this final portion. As you will quickly learn, our work is not all about technology. I hope you will find this last offering to be of value to you.

1. Do put a very high priority on relationships. Life is about how you interact with other people and with God. Don't be so absorbed in technology that you have no time for relationships with your family, your brethren, new converts, prospects, and most of all … with God!

   + If you are married, you have a wife. You are to be one with her, not with your iPhone.
   + You serve the living God, not your new Mac.
   + Your mission in life should involve teaching kids, not learning how to use your iPad.
   + You should seek the lost, not the latest upgrade from Microsoft.
   + You should control your technology; don't let it control you.

2. Do give attention to the person at the other end of your phone conversation. Don't email or browse the Internet while talking on the phone. Most folks on the other end will know you are distracted by something. You are not the king of multitasking.

3. Do speak clearly and distinctly when leaving a voicemail. Don't think the person listening to your message is good at deciphering mumbling. Old guys like Max may have to listen to a message ten times just to decipher the name! Give us a little help!

4. Do give complete attention when you are in important discussions. Don't do a mind-meld with your smart phone. Put it away; turn it off, out of reach, and out of sight. People (especially your wife) will appreciate the attention. You do not have to take every potential call that may come in. You are not Jack Bauer; the fate of the nation is not in your hands. If you must have your phone on during an important discussion, take the call only if it is from your sick mom or the president. All others can leave voicemail. That's what voicemail is for!

5. Do give attention to people even in casual conversations. Don't be distracted by your phone or computer when people come by to see you. Talking and eye contact are critical to relationships. If you try to carry on a conversation with someone while you are checking your email, don't be surprised if they feel slighted. If you don't have time for a casual visit in your office, then say so.

6. Do be practical in using technology. Don't think you have to have the latest tech stuff just because it is there. Think "tools," not "toys." Technology can be fun, but it has to have practical value in your work. If the church bought you a new iPad in 2010 (you should be so blessed!), do you need an upgrade to an iPad 3 this year?

7. Do work within a budget. Don't go in debt for tech. A Mac Pro starts at $2,500. With an 8-core processor, it starts at $3,500 (current, 2011). That would be a killer computer! But if you have to borrow the money, the debt may be the real killer! You do remember Proverbs 22:7, right?

8. Do understand that everybody else doesn't necessarily like your technology. Don't practice tech snobbery. You don't need to say to

other preachers, "My _____ (fill in the blank with computer, projector, or phone) is cooler than yours. You need to get one like mine." Have you ever thought that maybe he doesn't like yours, or can't afford yours?

9. Do practice your PowerPoint or Keynote presentations prior to preaching. Don't ever assume it will work without checking it first. A lot of preachers have been frustrated when they plugged their computers into the data projector only to have an unexpected glitch. Checking beforehand can avoid disastrous presentations.

10. Do research products carefully before purchasing a data projector. Don't think all projectors are created equal. For our purposes, LCD (Liquid Crystal Display) projectors typically give us the best balance between price and performance. But technology changes. What works well today will be replaced by something better tomorrow. LCOS (Liquid Crystal On Silicone) produces a spectacular image, but may not be as practical from a pricing perspective. DLP (Digital Light Processing) has high contrast ratios, but many preachers have been sorely disappointed with color quality. Yellows (an important highlighting color) on a DLP unit are not brilliant and bear a striking resemblance to dried mustard. A good consultant can help you find the right projector for your application. A number of preachers have been assisted by Lisa Phillips (*lisa@projectorpeople.com*) [used with permission]. She is among the best in the country at helping churches to economically get the best projector for their application.

11. Do set your projector up properly. Don't settle for a crooked or out-of-focus image. An image should fill the screen both vertically and horizontally. Why be picky about this kind of stuff? Because people don't buy sloppy work! "Good enough" is not good enough! If you are careless in your presentation work, maybe you are careless in your study! Don't leave that impression. By the way, don't expect a good image with a five-year-old bulb!

12. Do practice simplicity in your presentation graphics. Don't think that just anything you throw up on the screen is acceptable. Your graphics should please the eye; colors should not clash, and a multitude of fonts should not be used on a slide. I recommend that you avoid abbreviations of Bible books; it simply looks better to see the full name. Don't overuse features. Remember that PowerPoint is an aid; it is not the show. If you don't understand color coordination, go to NFL.com. Consultants are paid millions to come up with correct color combinations that teams use. Or, if you need help, talk to your wife or mom about color conflicts. A bright orange background combined with hot pink lettering doesn't work. Your wife will know that. Let her help.

13. Do limit the number of slides in your presentation. Don't think more is better! Using a large number of slides can actually limit understanding and retention. I have used slides (35mm and PowerPoint) for more than 35 years. By experience, I know what works. Strength is not found in numbers. Don't think you have to put every verse on your slides. You may think you have created a masterpiece by loading your slides with detail. Your audience will not think so. A variety of professional studies agree that less is more. An exception might be when you are showing photos (as in making a report on the work you did at Karnack, Egypt). Even then, limit yourself to about 20 photos. George Mason University has a good checklist for your slides at *http://mason.gmu.edu/~montecin/powerpoint.html* (current 2011). A presentation works well with a title, a reference to the main text, and the three points of the sermon. Simplicity sells! Professionals say too many slides is a mark of a novice. Don't look like a novice.

14. Do keep private conversations and conflicts to yourself. Don't ever, under any circumstances, take personal conflicts with anyone to Facebook or Twitter. Discourage others from doing so. People have

made some real messes by posting stuff they shouldn't.

15. Do exercise good judgment and self-control in the use of technology. Don't use idle time to just roam the Internet. An untold number of Christian men have found themselves where they should not be when they do that. The privacy of smart phones makes that especially dangerous. You may Google a word that seems harmless, but it leads to images that are not. Out of curiosity, you click on an image that seems harmless, but it leads to a website that is not. Out of curiosity, you explore that website; harmless is now gone. Idle time on the computer or smart phone may indeed lead you into the devil's workshop.

16. Do be honest, open, and pure in your texting. Don't ever text anything to anyone that could be construed as sexual or flirty. If you are married, every text you send or receive should absolutely be open to your wife. You have no right to claim privacy! I have known of many men (though not preachers) who thought they had a right to keep texts private from their wives. They did that because they had something to hide.

17. Do use the Internet to let people know about the church in your community. Yellow Pages are history. The Internet is the first place people go today when looking for a church. You don't have to have a fancy web page. But you need to have enough on it to give folks basic info about the church.

Indeed, technology presents challenges. Use it wisely for the benefit of the kingdom.

Young preacher, may these thoughts help you be what God wants you to be. I trust you are already on the right track on most of these things. You can have a great future ahead of you if you apply the wisdom presented here and in the rest of this book. I pray that you will be greatly used by our Lord, and that many lost souls will find their way home because of your diligent labor.

How to Keep Yourself Morally Pure
By David Banning

Sometimes I wish I could go back to the blissful ignorance of my youth. When I was a boy, a preacher's immorality would have been discussed by adults outside of my presence. I would have been completely unaware. Now … I know … and I don't like it.

It is with profound grief and sadness that I hear all too frequently about men devoted to preaching the gospel who allow themselves to be lured by Satan into immorality. I grieve over the irreparable harm that is done to their families. I have tried to console brethren who were disillusioned by this betrayal. I have labored with churches that were trying to recover and move the work of God forward in the aftermath of the scandal. Recovering from a preacher's fall is a painful, difficult process that sometimes takes years. It's happening too often. It should not be so!

There are many dimensions of this problem that could be explored. There are things that need to be said about why this happens and the terrible toll that it takes on families, brethren, and the cause of Christ generally. But our purpose is to address prevention. What can gospel preachers do to keep themselves morally pure, while doing the work of God in an immoral world? It will be my goal to avoid vague generalities in addressing this question and to offer instead some very practical suggestions. Brothers, as we preach the gospel we will wage a battle for our purity. We must win this battle!

Stay Close to God

It is certainly possible for a gospel preacher to become so consumed with his study, his work, and caring for the spiritual needs of others, that he begins to neglect his own relationship with his Lord. When this happens, we make ourselves vulnerable to Satan's assault. One preacher who became involved in criminal immorality and is now facing years in prison made this statement about his spiritual condition in the days leading up to his sin, "My faith wasn't as strong as I thought it was … I hadn't studied His word or prayed in months. I was so weak." Keep in mind that this man was still preaching, teaching, and performing all of his assigned tasks each week. But it was all a façade; his faith was in shambles. His tragic story is a powerful reminder of just how far a man can fall when he neglects his relationship with God.

It is precisely at this point that the solution to the problem of moral impurity begins. Gospel preachers (and for that matter, all disciples) must stay close to God. How this happens is not rocket science. We need to pray (Colossians 4:2; 1 Thessalonians 5:17). We need to have a daily habit of meaningful communication with God. We need to read the Bible (Psalm 119:9-11, 148). I'm not talking about the kind of reading preachers do to prepare for class or to put together a sermon outline. We need to spend time in the book every day, allowing God to speak to us and pondering the application of His words to our lives. It is a healthy exercise for preachers to follow a daily Bible reading schedule, just what we encourage others to do.

I would suggest getting to the church building early in the morning before the phone begins ringing and people begin to stop by. Before you begin working on sermons and class materials, block out some time to read your Bible and pray to God. Let it be the first thing you do every day. Victory in the battle for moral purity begins with a close, meaningful relationship between a man and his God.

Maintain a Strong Marriage

In Proverbs 5 Solomon begins to lay out the catastrophic consequences of adultery (Proverbs 5:1-14). To help a man avoid this pitfall, he points to marriage as the relationship where sexual desire is to be satisfied (Proverbs 5:15-20). It is our marriage then, which serves a vital part of our defense against moral impurity, particularly sexual sin. When marriages are healthy and needs are met, Satan will have a far more difficult time trying to lure a man or woman into sexual sin. But when marriages are dysfunctional and important needs are left unmet, people become far more susceptible to the devil's assault.

What happens in our marriages over the years becomes very important in this battle for our moral purity. We need to invest the time necessary to cultivate a strong bond with our wives. A careful study of the Song of Solomon will reveal at least four dimensions of the romantic love so vital to a marriage.

1. *Companionship* (Song of Solomon 1:15-2:13)—We need to spend time with our wives. We need to carve out time in our schedule, put others off to another time, and make the sacrifices necessary to be together. Make sure that you continue to date your wife. Thirty days should not pass without the two of you going out for an evening together or finding some other way to spend some quiet time alone.

2. *Communication* (Song of Solomon 6:4-9)—We need to talk to our wives. These conversations should involve much more than simply sharing schedules or arranging for someone to pick up the kids. We need to communicate our love and appreciation for our wives. We ought to have honest and open conversations about the state of our relationship and what aspects need some work. We need to be willing to hear her when she is trying to say, "You're spending too much time addressing the needs of others and not taking care of me."

3. *Caring* (Song of Solomon 1:1-14)—We need to take care of our wives. We must make it our ambition to understand her needs as a unique woman and become the expert at meeting those needs in ways that are important to her (1 Peter 3:7; Ephesians 5:25-33).

4. *Craving* (Song of Solomon 2:3-7)—When the first three dimensions exist in a marriage, the fourth will be the natural by-product. We will

crave physical intimacy with each other and be less inclined to look elsewhere.

No marriage will be perfect. Every couple will pass over some rough places in the road. But the key to a great marriage is to keep working at it. Do not allow yourself to be so caught up in your work with God's people that you neglect the most important person in your life. Make sure you take care of your wife and build a strong relationship with her. A strong marriage will serve as a key line of defense against moral impurity.

Don't Be Arrogant

On January 3, 1993 the Houston Oilers faced the Buffalo Bills in the AFC Wildcard game. They had easily beaten the Bills the previous week. Shortly after the third quarter began, the Oilers had a thirty two point lead! It appeared that they had the game won. But any fan of the Houston Oilers knows that this is not what happened. The Bills came back and won the game. It was the greatest comeback in playoff history. But how could it happen? How could a team with a thirty-two point lead in the third quarter lose the game? The answer is simple. The Oilers became arrogant. They thought they had the game won. They let down their guard.

It is this same kind of arrogant thinking that gets preachers into trouble. Some men come to believe that they are too strong, too spiritually mature to get caught up in immorality. As a result, they let down their guard. They put themselves in risky situations and make themselves vulnerable to Satan's assault. After being caught in adultery, one preacher confessed that he just thought he was too old to be caught up in something like this. He thought he had this battle won and he let down his guard.

It is arrogant and dangerous to allow ourselves to believe that we are beyond being tempted by immorality (Proverbs 16:18; 1 Corinthians 10:12). Don't ever say, "I could never commit adultery" or "I could never be involved in Internet pornography." It is wiser to believe that, because I can fall into sin, I need to be careful. I need to be on guard. I need to refrain from risky behavior. This brings us to our next line of defense against immorality.

Put Up Fences

Because I can succumb to temptation, I need to protect myself by putting up some fences. Put simply, if you don't want to become involved in immorality, don't put yourself in situations that make it possible (Proverbs 4:10-27; 5:8). Put up some fences. Make some rules for yourself that make it difficult to become involved in sexual sin. Let me share with you some of the "fences" we recommend to the young men in our preacher training program.

1. ***Don't be alone with other women.*** If you need to conduct a Bible study with a woman, take your wife, an elder, or one of the members with you. If that's not possible, postpone the study for another time. If one of the sisters is having trouble and needs to talk, make sure someone is with you. If a woman shows up at your office and wants to talk, arrange another time for you and your wife to come by and visit with her. This will not always be convenient and some may even be offended. But this is a small price to pay to protect your purity. Don't be pressured into compromising on this. The woman who insists on seeing you alone is the woman with whom you must not be alone!

2. ***Avoid becoming a marriage counselor.*** When a preacher privately counsels and comforts a woman who is angry and disappointed with her husband, he is asking for trouble. Put up a fence here! Encourage troubled couples to seek counsel from the shepherds of your congregation, or from an older, wiser couple. When you must handle these situations, insist that you talk with the husband and wife together and do it at a time when your wife can be with you.

3. ***Be careful about working relationships with other women.*** It is easy to
    find yourself partnered with some other woman in the congregation
    to work on a project together. It may be one of the ladies who is
    helping print the bulletin or assisting with a Bible class curriculum.
    Preachers can stumble into these situations without appreciating the
    danger. It is dangerous to spend hours working alone with another
    woman, even if it is a spiritual labor that you are doing at the church
    building. Put up a fence here! Turn this partnership into a team
    of several people. Get the whole group involved in completing this
    project.

4. ***Do not stay in homes where you will be alone with a woman.***
    Sometimes brethren are not sensitive about the awkward positions
    into which they put preachers. During a gospel meeting, you may find
    yourself in a home where the husband and kids leave in the morning
    and you are all alone with the wife. The best way to handle this
    situation is to anticipate it. I always try to ask in advance what my
    accommodations will be and, when necessary, request not to be put in
    that situation.

5. ***Use common sense with the Internet.*** One of the reasons so
    many men get into trouble on the Internet is because the wrong
    information is so easy to access, and it seems this can be done with
    anonymity. We need to put some fences up here! There are some
    simple, common sense things that can be done to avoid getting into
    trouble. First, try to do your Internet work in a more public setting
    and at a time when others are around. Keep your office door open.
    Take your laptop into the living room and respond to your email
    while family is around. Privacy is one of the things that gets men
    into trouble on the Internet. Try to eliminate that privacy. Second,
    give your wife complete access to your "Internet life." Never have a
    computer or email accounts that she is not able to access. Third, use

filtering software and set preferences in a way that will minimize the danger of accidentally stumbling across the wrong material. Fourth, be especially careful about your activities on social networking sites like Facebook. Sites like these have become a way for people to reconnect with old friends – sometimes old boyfriends and girlfriends from high school or college. In some cases, these renewed friendships have ignited old flames and led to adultery. The problem is so pervasive that some in the media are asking, "Does Facebook cause adultery?" For that reason, we need to be very careful about who we choose to connect with and what kind of messages we exchange with old friends. Make this an activity you share with your wife. I called these common sense suggestions. I suspect all godly men know that they ought to do things like this. Most preachers have given similar counsel to parents with teenagers. Sometimes we need to learn to follow our own advice.

Appreciate the Possibilities

When we read 2 Samuel 11, we are stunned by King David's behavior. David was a good man who knew the will of God. What was he thinking? How could he do this? Did he not realize that God knew what he was doing? Did he honestly think he could get away with this? These are the same questions that inevitably follow a preacher's moral collapse. It seems utterly bizarre that men who know God's word so well can become involved in behavior that is so clearly wrong (Matthew 5:27-28; Hebrews 13:4) and destructive (Proverbs 5:1-14). How does this happen?

Dr. Russell Moore made an interesting observation while commenting on a recent moral scandal involving one of our politicians. He said, "Temptation only works if the possible futures open to you are concealed. Consequences, including those of Judgment Day, must be hidden from view or outright denied." To become involved in immorality, a man must convince himself that somehow he will escape the consequences of his actions. He will not get caught. No one will find out. His marriage will not be ruined. His kids will not be harmed. He will be able to continue preaching. This kind of thinking seems completely irrational. And yet it is exactly the kind of deluded mindset that takes over when a man caves to his lust and becomes involved in immorality. He simply refuses to see the catastrophe that is coming.

If David just could have seen the dreadful future he faced because of his sin with Bathsheba, perhaps he would have made a different choice that night on the rooftop in Jerusalem. If we could see the devastation that moral impurity can bring into our lives, perhaps we would make different choices. My co-worker urges young men to look at today's decisions with tomorrow's eyes. We regularly rehearse with the young men in our training program all of the terrible things that can happen when a preacher becomes involved in immorality. These conversations not only help these young men, they help me too. They help me see today's decisions with tomorrow's eyes. They help me look beyond the moment and consider the consequences of my actions. Appreciating the possibilities becomes a powerful line of defense against temptation.

Find Someone To Hold You Accountable

I remember reading a few years ago about a man who met every month with an older friend in the congregation he attended. He had given this friend permission to ask him some very direct, personal questions every time they met. When they finished lunch, his friend would ask, "Have you been faithful to your wife over the last thirty days?" "Have your Internet activities been pure for the last month?" "Have your thoughts and motives been pure as you interacted with other women?" This man knew that every month he would meet with his old friend and answer these questions. As you can imagine, this kind of accountability serves as a powerful deterrent against sin. When confronted with temptation, this guy knew that, if he gave in, he would face a crisis before thirty days passed. His friend was going to ask those questions and he would be forced to lie or confess.

Finding someone to hold you accountable is especially important for men who struggle with pornography. The accessibility of explicit material and the opportunity to view it with anonymity makes it easy for men to slip back into the sin again and again. Knowing that someone is going to ask becomes a powerful incentive to do the right thing at the moment of temptation.

I would offer this word of caution. Preachers need to be very careful when selecting an accountability partner. It needs to be someone who will be faithful to do this over the long haul; someone with the strength to ask tough questions; someone you can trust not to betray your confidence. You should choose someone older than yourself and preferably someone who worships at another place. Some men find that fathers are an excellent choice.

A Final Thought

It is easy to pass lightly over admonitions to protect our purity when the possibility of falling into sexual sin seems remote. I fear that there are some who will read this who have not yet faced an intense assault on their purity. As a result, they may consider some of the practical admonitions to be extreme and unnecessary. Don't make that mistake. The assault on our purity is real. Our enemy is crafty. The potential damage is incalculable. We have seen too many men succumb to this temptation. It's time for gospel preachers to get serious about this battle and do what we must to protect our purity.

Dear Young Preacher
From Brent Lewis

Preaching is not just about speaking, skill, oratory. It is about living and loving the cause of Christ. And if you are not living at all times in a way that will serve the Lord Jesus Christ, your preaching will be a disaster.

You have embarked on the most important work a person can do in life—preaching the truth that will save men's souls. That doesn't necessarily make you an important person; it just means you are engaged in important work. In fact, there can be nothing more compelling and rewarding.

You will need help along the way. Particularly, you will need help from the Lord. So pray sincerely and often that the Lord will enable you to be effective in your preaching and helpful to the brethren with whom you work. Keep a humble, open, compliant attitude toward yourself and others.

Most young preachers have things to learn to improve their effectiveness. Be willing to learn; be determined to improve—both methods and material.

If you are an avid reader and careful student of the Scriptures, you will never run out of material to preach. One of the most amazing things about God's word is that we can continue to learn new lessons and see new applications almost every time we get into it. Read the Bible more than you read other books. As you read, ideas will come for subjects to pursue. Each time you read, you will get something you didn't get before. Plus, you will become more familiar with the text itself—which will make you better able to understand it, teach it, live it, and bring it to mind when needed.

It is my judgment that it would be wise to read other books. Extensive reading, even of things like history, will certainly enhance your overall knowledge and help you communicate with others. I would particularly recommend that you read good books written by New Testament Christians to enhance and broaden your base of knowledge. You might want to read some of the classic Restoration literature. You will likely want to use Bible commentaries at various times. But keeping a good balance is always important in any area, so in your study, you'll need to find a balance between using commentaries as a crutch and refusing to learn from godly men who may have excellent insights into the Scripture.

Your subjects need to be fresh, or maybe freshly approached, but they don't need to be new. Men and women are basically the same today as they were 100 years ago, or 2000 years ago. Human nature doesn't change, and thus the gospel doesn't need to either. Think long and hard about preaching something new and revolutionary that you've never heard expressed. Talk with a mentor or seasoned preacher about it before you do. It's not likely you're going to discover some new doctrine or new truth.

Don't try to be something or someone you're not. You may admire someone else's preaching style, but you need to develop your own without mimicking someone else's. You can certainly pick up some effective traits from other good preachers, but don't try to act and sound just like them. Be yourself.

If you are not married, ask the Lord to help you pick a good spouse. The congregation is not hiring your wife, but she will be a vital part of any work you do with them. Your wife will either help you or hurt you in that work. You need someone who will help you by being treasured and appreciated and loved for who she is. I can tell you that anytime I have decided to leave a congregation to go work somewhere else, the brethren have made it clear that they hate to lose my wife every bit as much (probably more, if the truth were known) as they hate to lose me. That's a great situation to have. Just be advised that your wife will either help you, or hinder you, in your work.

Work on your strengths as well as your weaknesses. Your wife can be a big help with this. You need a wife or some friend who will be totally honest with you to help you keep improving. If you're like most of us, you will need to eliminate some habits or mannerisms that may distract from the message and inhibit your effectiveness.

Sharpen your tools. Work on your strengths as well as your weaknesses. Determine to use the English language properly. Many years ago, I knew a preacher who told on himself that he'd had a lady come out after the sermon and tell him he'd made (something like) 32 grammatical errors in his sermon. I think they were mostly "double negatives" because he was particularly bad about using those. When he told a group of preachers about this, one of them said, "What did you say to her?" He said (and I promise this is the truth), "I never said nothin'. I was afraid I'd make another'n." Bad habits—grammar, mannerisms, or otherwise—will limit your effectiveness. You don't want people concentrating on your errors instead of your message.

Understand at all times that who you are is every bit as important (if not more so) than what you preach. There is an old saying about one who preached (who shouldn't have) that goes something like this: "When he got into the pulpit, you'd think it was a shame he would ever come out. But when he got out of the pulpit, you'd think it was a shame he should ever go back in." You get the drift. Preaching is not just about speaking, skill, oratory. It is about living and loving the cause of Christ. And if you are not living at all times in a way that will serve the Lord Jesus Christ, your preaching will be a disaster.

You may have success as a preacher from the standpoint of compliments from others. Be grateful for them but take them with "a grain of salt." I've often said that no preacher is ever as good as the brethren sometimes make him out to be. Maintain a malleable and teachable spirit and attitude. Don't have a haughty or competitive spirit. Know what and for whom you're preaching. It is not for fame or popularity; it is for Jesus and the truth. Know who you're trying to please—not the audience, but the Lord.

When you're preaching for and working with a congregation, you'll need to learn to be both bold and loving at the same time. You will need to reprove and exhort. But don't be overly critical of brethren. They are humans and they will make mistakes. Don't whine or complain about yourself or the brethren. It will discourage others, and you need to be in the business of encouraging, not discouraging.

Please understand and be keenly aware that Satan has his special ways to attack preachers: primarily, pride, discouragement, sex, laziness, and fear. Determine that you will know (and acknowledge to yourself) your weaknesses—and pray, pray, pray that the Lord will deliver you from temptation to any of these.

Maintain your enthusiasm for what you are doing, and never lose it. You are engaged in the most important work that a man can do: the salvation of souls. You are a servant, ministering the word of Christ to others, and by doing so will build up, strengthen, and bring to greater knowledge both those who are longing to know, and those who have come to know the Lord Jesus Christ. Preach the word, brother!

How to Deal Wisely with Elders
By Jon W. Quinn

I suppose if I were going to sum up the work of the preacher, I could do no better than to echo the words that were among the last recorded by the apostle Paul. These were written to a preacher named Timothy. Paul solemnly charged Timothy in the presence of God and of Jesus Christ, "Preach the word; be ready in season and out of season; reprove, rebuke, exhort, with great patience and instruction" (2 Timothy 4:2).

It is a wonderful privilege and a great blessing for any preacher, young or old, to be able to work with godly and responsible elders. When both the preacher and the elders love the Lord and seek to exalt and honor Him in their work, there will be synergy created by God in that work. There will also develop a deep love and respect for one another as fellow laborers in the most important endeavor of all—assisting others in their relationships with the King and in their attaining an everlasting inheritance. Recall the tender moments at Miletus as Paul was passing through, spending brief, but precious moments with the elders from Ephesus. They had shared so much in their three years of working together earlier in Paul's ministry. How poignant were the tears of sorrow at their parting, perhaps never to see one another again. And yet, that sorrow had a sweet side to it. It was made possible by their appreciation, love, and joy in one another (Acts 20:17-38). How wonderful it would be if every preacher of the gospel would be able to develop this kind of relationship with godly elders!

Defining Godly Leadership

When talking of leadership, perhaps the greatest need is to realize that a good leader in the local church will be an accurate example of what a Christian ought to be. Paul counseled Timothy "…in speech, conduct, love, faith and purity, show yourself an example of those who believe"(1 Timothy 4:12). Timothy was to lead by example and no one should be imitated if his example is not worthy of imitation! A good spiritual leader is one who understands that he is a servant, first of Christ and then to others. Words such as "gentle" and "patient" come to mind. Elders and preachers need to have the mind of Christ.

An elder has been appointed to his position because he has shown himself to possess good spiritual qualities. This assumes that the church where he has been appointed has taken seriously those characteristics a man is required to have to be approved by God for such a task (1 Timothy 3:1-7; Titus 1:5-9). These brethren will be men of experience and proven faith with high standards of personal conduct and great love for the Lord. They will be men of prayer, compassion, and dedication as they attend to the nurturing process of feeding the souls of the flock among them.

A *preacher* is one who "heralds," or makes a public proclamation of, the gospel of the Lord Jesus Christ. He is a messenger of the good news. This is but one aspect of *"feeding the flock"* and thus overlaps with the elders' work and responsibility. A preacher may be an older man who has proven himself much in the same way as an elder has, or he may be a young man who is in the process of gaining experience. In either case, he also needs to have great faith, an unquenchable love for the Lord and a high standard of personal conduct.

So, the work and responsibility of elders and preachers overlap, but they are not the same, and it is not a competition. Elders and preachers are meant to assist one another to meet the challenges of faith together and mutually assist one another in bringing glory to God. It is much the same as Jethro once counseled his son-in-law whom God had appointed to lead Israel to the Promised Land. He told Moses, "You will surely wear out, both yourself and these people who are with you, for the task is too heavy for you; you cannot do it alone" (Exodus 18:18). He then advised Moses, "Furthermore, you shall select out of all the people able men who fear God, men of truth, those who hate dishonest gain; and you shall place these over them as leaders of thousands, of hundreds, of fifties and of tens" (Exodus 18:21). Godly elders will certainly help keep the young preacher from being overwhelmed or burdened excessively. It is a wise preacher who recognizes the benefits of working with godly elders and learns to depend on them for encouragement and guidance in accomplishing their mutual responsibility of building up the saints.

The Ideal

It is so critical that the hearts of both the elders and the preacher be fully dedicated to the primary goal of bringing God glory. Even men with great natural ability can do much harm to the work when such abilities are not controlled by godly traits. One necessary step in dealing wisely with elders is for the preacher, with his heart renewed by the gospel of grace and his mind set on the Spirit, to pursue those things which are pleasing to God. The elders should be able to have confidence in the preacher that he will do everything he can to assist them in carrying out their responsibilities to the Lord, whether the present circumstances require reproof, rebuke, or exhortation.

The goal of all instruction is stated by Paul in 1 Timothy 1:5, "But the goal of our instruction is love from a pure heart and a good conscience and a sincere faith." The Hebrew writer urged, "Obey your leaders and submit to them, for they keep watch over your souls as those who will give an account. Let them do this with joy and not with grief, for this would be unprofitable for you" (Hebrews 13:17). A preacher with the right goal and a correct view of the responsibilities of the elders to the church, and the church to the elders, is going to put forth the required effort to make this ideal the reality. Paul wrote to the Thessalonians, "But we request of you, brethren, that you appreciate those who diligently labor among you, and have charge over you in the Lord and give you instruction, and that you esteem them very highly in love because of their work. Live in peace with one another" (1 Thessalonians 5:12-13). Godly elders are most certainly going to appreciate this assistance and thank God for the preacher's efforts as he exhorts the brethren to do as these verses suggest. The church will prosper and God will be glorified.

When Things Are Less Than Ideal

Understand, if one looks hard enough, he can find imperfections in the most faithful and noblest of men. I fear that sometimes a preacher may become disillusioned because he has found a flaw in one of the elders. But we ought not to expect that we will ever meet a flawless man. We all have flaws. The more we come to know another man, the more likely that we will discover some of them. God knows that, and yet He still has said that he wants some of us to be elders in local churches. A flaw discovered in a man does not mean that he does not have his mind set on the Spirit, and it does not mean that he is not qualified to be an elder, or that he does not deserve patient, loving and respectful support. An elder has as much right to "press on toward perfection" and to "work out his own salvation" as does anyone else. It is not in perfection, but rather in a man's sincere determination to reach toward perfection that gives evidence of his spiritual strength and commitment to Jesus. One must not make too much out of such flaws when they are found.

While we are all *works in progress*, there is still that man whose mind is "set on the Spirit" in contrast to the mind "set on the flesh." But what does a spiritually minded preacher do when an elder or elders fall short of the ideal to the degree of potentially hurting the work and perhaps even endangering the souls of others?

I believe that pride is often the carnal villain that is behind problems that will sometimes arise between preachers and elders, and among brethren in general. Sometimes it becomes a "turf war" where factions vie for territory. But, honestly now, when such has happened is it not because some have forgotten that their purpose is to glorify God? That should always be the focus of every preacher, and be evident in all of his actions, speech, and prayers. Always!

If there is a prideful abuse of power on the part of an elder, and it can and does happen, what does the preacher do then? Hurtful things can be said that could have long lasting effects. The church and the work suffer. The preacher can do no better than to get on his knees before God and promise that he will do all he can to unconditionally subject himself to the Lord's will in everything. He will be an example of faith and righteous conduct. He will be fair and patient. He will not allow things to escalate by returning evil for evil and insult for insult (Romans 12:17, 1 Peter 3:9).

That said, there are going to be rough times ahead, as there always is when the carnality of man is permitted to affect our behavior. It is almost certain that any young (or old) preacher with an appropriate measure of humility and understanding will be conflicted and perhaps intimidated by such a challenge. But he is a gospel preacher. Though his heart may be heavy, he is to preach the word in season and out of season. His Lord is in heaven and He is the King we serve. Having determined to say and do nothing that would not please the Lord, and with much prayer and genuine love for all, as gently (that is, with "controlled strength") as possible, the issues must be confronted.

The Scriptures do give instruction concerning this situation. First, if it is a matter of an accusation made against an elder, let there be two or three witnesses. This helps to assure that it is a true and just accusation. If there is sin, give the elder time and opportunity to repent. Try to work it out with him in a brotherly fashion (1 Timothy 5:1). If he continues in sin, then there will be the need for a more public approach and rebuke. A preacher must be even-handed in his approach to these kinds of things. He must never, ever show partiality in the way he reacts to sin. The Lord expects the preacher to treat a close friend the same as he would treat anyone else (1 Timothy 5:19-21).

The Preacher's Responsibility

A preacher needs to be an example of faith in everything. I can do no better, nor be any wiser in my approach to my relationship with the elders, than to give attention to developing strong, spiritual, Christ-like character traits in myself. There is only one way to do this, and that is through application. Excuses are often offered for not doing so. A brother or sister will admit that perhaps how they have dealt with an issue was not entirely right but the circumstances permitted them to make an exception "just this once" and deal with it in their own way rather than the Lord's way. This is a sadly common, inaccurate and spiritually immature perspective on true discipleship. I could spend all day justifying less than spiritual behavior on my part, but at the end of the day "… it is not he who commends himself that is approved, but he whom the Lord commends" (2 Corinthians 10:18).

Every decision we make develops character of some sort in some way. We simply cannot afford the luxury of ever putting noble and spiritual ideals aside, even for a moment, whatever the provocation. After Paul had urged Timothy to show himself an example of those who believe, he continued, "Take pains with these things; be absorbed in them, so that your progress will be evident to all. Pay close attention to yourself and to your teaching; persevere in these things, for as you do this you will ensure salvation both for yourself and for those who hear you" (1 Timothy 4:15-16).

The phrases *"take pains with these things"* and *"be absorbed in them"* speak volumes about a preacher's dedication to his, and others', spiritual progress. As the preacher develops his working relationship with the elders, he needs to be intensely focused on being God's man rather than his own man. Let it be that at day's end my actions and words have been those that the Lord commends and approves.

A preacher needs humility in his relationship with the elders. The elders I work with need to know that I respect their work and their position. They are where they are by the Lord's own design. As a preacher, my disposition toward them needs to be one of genuine esteem. They should see it in my words and actions. Even my body language ought to reveal the seriousness with which I view our relationship, not because they are my lords, but because I am the Lord's.

One way I can do my part is to remember what leadership is all about in the Kingdom of Christ. The true measure of greatness of leadership is determined not by personal status, popularity, or power, but in how diligently I serve others. It is not how high I can exalt myself, but rather, the extent to which I am willing to serve (Matthew 23:10-12).

A preacher should feel free to communicate his thoughts to the elders. If a preacher is aware of some matter that needs tending to, then the elders need to know about it. If the preacher has a promising idea that may help the work to grow, the elders ought to be a great sounding board. If the preacher is disappointed in the progress of the work, then that is a thing to discuss with the elders in a brotherly fashion. If the preacher should have a different judgment about a matter that the elders have reached, then he should feel free to respectfully communicate such to the elders, and the elders should be the kind of leaders that the preacher, or any member of the flock, would feel comfortable in doing so.

Also, when the preacher sees difficult work being done by the elders, he should encourage and support them. When he sees efforts that result in joyful success, the preacher should communicate his genuine appreciation for his pastors and their work. A preacher should be a "Son of Encouragement" like Barnabas every opportunity he gets. This encouragement could come in many forms. For example, if an elder is teaching a class on a certain subject, and the preacher has a book recommendation or helpful study material in mind that might benefit the elder's teaching, this would be a good time to share this helpful information with the elder.

A preacher needs a strong conviction that the New Testament is an adequate guide on how he is to deal with the elders. I, frankly, have experienced times where I found myself wishing the Bible said more or perhaps addressed more precisely the current troublesome situation that I am facing. I have always taught that the New Testament is an adequate guide and authority for living by faith. If that is so, then it is adequate when it comes to the preacher dealing with the elders.

I am convinced that a spiritual, knowledgeable man, with prayer and honest evaluation, can take the principles provided in our Covenant and come to a sound, spiritual conclusion, even when specifics are not to be found. It is not that the needed instructions are absent or incomplete, but rather that the Scriptures often lay down holy and righteous principles that are meant to be applied to many situations. For example, we are told "Be devoted to one another in brotherly love; give preference to one another in honor" (Romans 12:10). Though not specifically about my relationship with elders, but rather with all brethren, it most certainly applies to how I deal with my brethren who are also elders.

So, in addition to obeying the word with reference to the specifics about elders and preachers and their work and relationship, I need to apply these more general teachings as well. It is only then that I will see the adequacy of the New Testament as a guide to my dealing wisely with the elders.

Concluding Thoughts

The key to successful faith in all things is love for the Lord Jesus and a resulting commitment to honor Him in all things. When a preacher sits down with his elders, he is sitting down with men that are better than he is. I use the term "better" in the sense of perspective, not actual worth. It is about having the mind of Christ toward others, including the elders, in my dealings with them. Paul wrote, "Do nothing from selfishness or empty conceit, but with humility of mind regard one another as more important than yourselves; do not merely look out for your own personal interests, but also for the interests of others. Have this attitude in yourselves which was also in Christ Jesus" (Philippians 2:3-5).

Let serving the Lord be the focus. Accept and be thankful for the assistance God gives you if you are a preacher blessed to work with spiritual and godly shepherds, not perfect men, but men being perfected even as you are being perfected in Christ, the Redeemer and Chief Shepherd of us all.

Dear Young Preacher
From Harry Pickup

Our duty is to declare what God has said;
this is where life-changing power is.

First, I would like to compliment you on choosing preaching as your "ministry in the Lord." You have put yourself in good company. Your service is a very important one. I hesitate to rank the various ministries in Christ because each one was chosen by Him and is, therefore, very important.

It is important to recall that one enters the ministry at the time he becomes a disciple. Just as when you obeyed the gospel so you also became a member of Christ's body. So, as you were redeemed from sin and reconciled to God you also became a "minister of Christ." All of His "ministries" are personal in their essence and are "fulfilled" individually. They cannot be "fulfilled" by proxy.

They must be "served" with considerable care which is continual in its nature. They are charged to "fulfill it" to the best of their ability. Note Paul's charge in the Colossian letter to Archippus (3:17): "And say to Archippus …"

The New Testament Scriptures explain clearly by the use of four words what the duty of the evangelist is. ***The first word, and the one probably most often used, is "gospel."*** This word means, "good news." "News" refers to things which have happened. "Good" defines the salutary effect it has upon the believing hearers.

The second word is "preach." It means a "public proclamation" and refers to the authority of another. In the days before modern means to make known generally the authority of a king, for example, the representative declared in a public place what was authorized. Authorization is necessary for obedience.

The third word is "teach." Teaching contains three elements: to inform, to interpret, to demonstrate relevance for living. The evangelist declares what the authority has authorized; he then explains its meaning and shows the effect in the believer's life.

The fourth word is "reason." This word means to ponder, to dispute with another. It is set in the context where hearers disagree with the speaker. It was used prominently by the Holy Spirit in reference to Paul's third evangelistic journey.

A careful study of these words in their special setting will clearly demonstrate, my younger brother, what your duties are.

You should recall always that you are a spokesman for another. And, that the ultimate object of your duty is to offer to sinful men the hope of salvation. Your influence upon your hearers does not come from your own scholarship or ability. It comes from your presenting soundly what God, the authority, has given you to say.

My personal study leads me to say there are three important words that will help the evangelist to do his duty: to think conceptually, to conclude carefully, to apply plainly. A *concept* is a mental picture that is drawn from the text that constitutes the will of God. A *conclusion* is a true statement drawn correctly from the concept. An *application* is the affect the first two words intend to have upon the obedient believer.

The idea behind these words makes the evangelist's duty sound and true according to the truth. They make the message understandable and expose any other teaching as error. They help avoid the speaker as appearing to be the authority, as well as being responsible for the thing taught. They prevent personal pride and discourage egotism.

It is very important for you to teach contextually. Keep in mind that there are three contexts to your preaching. The broadest context is the purpose of the entire inspired Scripture. (Ponder Ephesians 3:8-

11). Second, while all Scriptures are "inspired of God," various sections address particular circumstances including a variety of cultures. Make sure your preaching addresses the same circumstances that the original text does. Finally, your comments need to conform to the most limited passage you are discussing.

Every passage of Scripture has a particular meaning in its own context. It is never wise to explain meanings first by going to another passage using the same or similar words. Following these thoughts helps avoid the common mistake of "proof-texting." To illustrate: "For by grace have you been saved through faith" (Ephesians 2:8) has a meaning in that context regardless of what James 2:18-26 teaches. And again, while Romans 6:4 teaches that baptism is an immersion, that is not why it was written. It was written to show how being united with Christ has an important effect upon the obedient believer. Scriptures do prove arguments; they do that according to the purpose of the particular writing.

Ideas are expressed in words. Therefore, words are important. It is important to study the meanings of words as well as their grammatical use. The strongest words in sentences are verbs. Learning meanings and grammar are not the same as translating. The neophyte in word studies and grammar is not qualified as a scholar.

Figures of speech are useful in sharpening one's understanding. They beautify and make ideas attracting. They are never as helpful, however, as words used literally. To illustrate: it is common knowledge that there are three words which are used to denote those who "lead" a congregation: "elder, bishop and pastor." The last two are metaphors; the first word has a literal meaning. It speaks to age and experience which lead to maturity. It is the stronger word of the three. To communicate, interpret, and apply ideas soundly it is important to understand words and their meanings through use.

One can learn about preaching from many books of the Bible. In my judgment, 1 Timothy 4 is the most comprehensive passage concerning the preacher's responsibility in the entire New Testament Scriptures. It includes instruction on how to build his message, how to develop his character, how to present the message, the plain contrast of truth and error. And, you can learn how to influence hearers to obey the teaching and inspiration for their continual growth. Also, in my judgment, it would be wise for each evangelist to memorize this passage so that it is continual in his mind as he preaches.

Paul, the prince of preachers, demonstrates his familiarity with uninspired, though wise writings. Occasionally he mentions them in his writings. This justifies our moderate use of such sources in our modern day preaching.

In this regard, reference materials are the best source of additional help. Various word studies are also good. However, care should be given that one does not appear scholarly beyond his knowledge and ability. Understanding the culture of the people addressed is also important. While men do not vary in their nature their circumstances do. To ignore this can cause one to appear ignorant.

One's thinking can be helped by consulting writers who respect the Scriptures as God's word and whose comments demonstrate an attempt to explain a meaning consistent with what the text says. First, however, one should consult men who are responsible Christians because they are more apt to understand God's revealed purpose. There is a danger in reading any human commentary; the danger is increased when one is reading denominational comments. Diligence and care should be used when consulting such writings.

Historical writings are good for comparative purposes. One needs to be sure that history is saying what happened, rather than being a commentary on what happened.

One is always influenced by events which occur in his living. First, remember the most important influence comes from divine testimony or facts and truth. Illustrations are helpful in explaining testimony but they are never equal to it. For this reason I feel that illustrations should follow the presentation of divine testimony.

We must never lose sight of our hearers and the reason we are speaking to them. Our duty is to declare what God has said; this is where life-changing power is. It is not in one's wisdom, scholarship, or ability.

Read, ponder, and practice. I wish you well in your noble calling. I am available for help.

How to Do Personal Evangelism
By Mike Wilson

Preachers come in all shapes and sizes. They also have vast differences in personality, educational achievement, and skill sets. However, if they are true evangelists, there is one thing they have in common—*the work of evangelism*. Paul's charge is to "do the work of an evangelist, fulfill your ministry" (2 Timothy 4:5). What is this work? A cursory look at 1 & 2 Timothy and Titus shows that an evangelist's role is to *save the lost* and *edify the saved*.

Evangelism and edification are two sides of the same coin. Evangelists work with others to "equip the saints for the work of ministry, for building up the body of Christ" (Ephesians 4:11-12). Successful evangelists will not only do the work themselves but teach others how to do it. "And what you have heard from me in the presence of many witnesses entrust to faithful men who will be able to teach others also" (2 Timothy 2:2). In order to effectively train and mentor others, there must be a core competency of the process involved. We cannot show the way if we do not lead by example.

Get Motivated

Achievement in evangelism, like many other noble endeavors, is 1% perspiration and 99% motivation. Jesus was motivated. He said of His own mission, "For the Son of Man came to seek and to save the lost" (Luke 19:10). Jeremiah was motivated. Tempted to give up in the face of relentless assaults, he expressed resolute determination to go on: "If I say, 'I will not mention him, or speak any more in his name,' there is in my heart as it were a burning fire shut up in my bones, and I am weary with holding it in, and I cannot" (Jeremiah 20:9). The apostle Paul was motivated. He said, "Therefore knowing the fear of the Lord, we persuade others… Therefore, we are ambassadors for Christ, God making his appeal through us. We implore you on behalf of Christ, be reconciled to God" (2 Corinthians 5:11a, 20).

Motivation must be deep-seated and profound if we are to endure constant rejection and overcome natural fears in an effort to find another lost soul who will listen to the good news. The guiding principle, or driving force, to do this work is embedded in the Great Commission (Matthew 28:18-20). The charge assumes three things: 1) people are lost in sin; 2) the gospel of Christ is the only means of rescuing them; and 3) if we don't share the message of salvation with them, who will? The hardest-working evangelists I know have an acute awareness of these truths, and they take them to heart.

Ask For Help

Sometimes preachers are tempted to think more highly of themselves than they ought to think, and this limits their usefulness. Swallow your pride and ask questions of others who are doing evangelism well. This is especially important after you develop a general approach to teaching the lost. Don't limit yourself to one system or method. There are good men and women who can teach us a lot about how to reach lost souls if we are humble enough to ask the right questions. Make this an area of your vocation in which you are committed to life-long learning and continual improvement, so that "your latter works exceed the first" (Revelation 2:19).

More importantly, ask God for help. J. Hudson Taylor said, "When God's work is done in God's way for God's glory, it will never lack God's supply." I do a series of sermons on evangelism, and one of the lessons is entitled, "The Role of Prayer in Evangelism." Have you noticed how much the apostles depended on the Lord to open doors in the book of Acts? "Prayer" and "the ministry of the word" go together (Acts 6:4). The following categories of prayer can transform your evangelistic success.

+ Courage (Romans 1:16; 2 Timothy 1:7-8, 12; 2:8-10; Acts 4:29-31; 5:41-42)
+ Wisdom (Proverbs 11:30; 1 Corinthians 9:22; James 1:5; Colossians 4:5-6)
+ Opportunities (John 4:35; Proverbs 16:3; Colossians 4:2-4)
+ Evangelists (Luke 10:2; 2 Thessalonians 3:1-2; Ephesians 6:18-20)
+ Political Conditions (1 Timothy 2:1-4)
+ Lost Souls (Romans 10:1)

In 1 Corinthians 3:6, Paul says, "I planted, Apollos watered, but God gave the growth." When all is said and done and the Lord blesses you with some success, make sure to remember to give credit to whom credit is due.

Look For Prospects

Where do you find lost souls to teach? Everywhere! They include personal friends, relatives, neighbors, people with whom you do business, and parents of your children's friends. It could be your insurance agent, your realtor, your doctor, your dental hygienist, your pharmacist, your veterinarian, your banker, your barber, a waitress at your favorite restaurant, other parents connected to your child's sports team, your auto mechanic, or the checkout clerk you often see at the grocery store. *Every lost soul is fair game.* Develop a good business card and pass it out to everyone. Find a hobby and join a group of people with a common interest so you can meet some new contacts.

Constantly remind your brothers and sisters in Christ that you want to teach people about Jesus, and that you need their help. Ask them for references and urge them to bring you someone to teach. Cultivate an atmosphere in the local church in which others are constantly looking for promising contacts for you.

Pay special attention to visitors to church assemblies and Bible classes. They have a built-in interest. Treat them as honored guests, and make sure you respond to them. Esteem them as VIP prospects. As you begin the process of following up with your contacts, make sure to "pray without ceasing" (1 Thessalonians 5:17).

Cultivate Relationships

There are many techniques that one can use in working with people —including *what to say* and *how to say it*—but the key is to genuinely love those whom God sends our way. There is truth to the old adage, "People won't care how much you know until they know how much you care." In a world full of hurtful evils, love draws people like a powerful magnet. Show genuine interest in others, and depend on God to open doors, and you will find people to teach. Be a Good Samaritan who will practice the Golden Rule.

All of this requires a personal investment of time and energy. People will respond more favorably to the overtures of a patient friend than the polished presentation of one who comes off like a relentless salesman. In doing evangelistic work, we must remember that people are not robots. Part of our task is removing obstacles to a fair hearing of the message. Try to put yourself in the shoes of your prospects and imagine what prejudices they may have against the truth. Is there some way in which you can reduce the psychological distance on the road they must travel toward obedience to the gospel, without in any way compromising the message? Paul says, "To the weak I became weak, that I might win the weak. I have become all things to all people, that by all means I might save some" (1 Corinthians 9:22). Find some common ground and speak the cultural language of your prospects as best as you can.

Make It A Team Effort

TEAM stands for "**T**ogether **E**veryone **A**ccomplishes **M**ore." Local churches that build an evangelistic culture are usually far more successful at winning the lost than those that don't. Your influence for good will go much farther if this work is not limited to a one-man show. Teams have something that individuals do not have: *synergy*. A 60-watt light bulb has about the same number of photons as a medium-power laser beam, but in the laser beam they are more concentrated. Likewise, the individual strands of a rope are fragile before the manufacturing process intertwines them into a strong cord that is nearly unbreakable. "Two are better than one, because they have a good reward for their toil" (Ecclesiastes 4:9).

The New Testament contains many examples of *personal* evangelism, but it also is full of examples of *teamwork* in evangelism. Jesus sent out disciples two by two (Luke 10:1-2). Paul often went with others on his preaching journeys (cf. Acts 20:4). Barnabas and later Silas were partners in Paul's work (Acts 13:2; 15:39-40). And Paul says of John Mark, who had disappointed him on the first journey (Acts 13-14), that he later proved "useful to me for ministry" (2 Timothy 4:11).

There are a number of ways of developing evangelistic teamwork in the local church, but here are a few suggestions:

1. *Mentoring.* When you do personal evangelistic studies, take a capable brother with you. On-the-job training is the best classroom, and you will multiply your influence for good. At the end of each session, talk about what happened, how certain points were made, and what you might do better next time. Pray together, asking God to bless your efforts.

2. *Small home study groups.* As our culture becomes more secular, many people who would not be agreeable to visiting a church assembly *will* accept an invitation to a private home. Work with a group of Christians to develop a "neighborhood Bible study" in which brothers and sisters have a defined role in advance. The roles may vary: teachers, co-teachers, hosts, those who will pray, inviters, people persons who will "connect" with visitors, babysitters, etc. Whatever the role each member has, a team of Christians is doing evangelism together. Develop a colorful flyer that everyone can pass out to friends and relatives, and promote this as a "faith-building Bible discussion" with "opportunity for prayer requests" and "a chance to meet friendly people who love God and one another." For several years, I have

worked with other Christians in such classes on a monthly basis, so no one is over-committed. It is a non-threatening entry point or gateway to evangelism in which legitimate truth-seekers are identified and channeled into personal studies in which many eventually convert to Christ. Teachers should keep lecturing to a minimum and ask questions to foster discussion. Christians are able to share their faith in an intimate setting. At the end of the study, have a pre-designated brother collect prayer requests for what often becomes a passionately expressed prayer. Finally, reserve some "social interaction" time after the study is over. During such small group sessions, I have seen walls of resistance come down as lost people open up to the gospel.

3. *Gospel meetings focusing on visitors.* Try creating a venue that is totally geared toward "honored guests" instead of the needs of members. It may be a short series or even a single assembly. Do not call it a "gospel meeting," because that is "insider language" they won't understand. Find a need that resonates with the community, and use it as an opportunity to introduce people to the gospel. Here are some examples: *Where is Your Life Headed?*, *Help for Parents in a Troubled World*, *God and Science*, *What a Medical Doctor Said about Jesus*, and *Worry-Free Living in a Troubled Economy*. Have a team of greeters in the lobby with personal name badges (no titles) welcoming guests and passing out clipboards which contain an introductory flyer and a guest registration sheet that says "Welcome" on top. Minimize "insider" announcements. If you are going to use a capable preacher who will connect well with such an audience and make an impression, you should also use your best prayer leaders and song leaders. Song leaders should lead upbeat songs, relevant to the theme and with minimal archaic language, that are easy for guests to sing. An organized follow-up team should be in place prior to the event. Also, there is a need to "talk it up" and pray about it for at least a month or

two prior to the meeting so that every member is excited about it and eager to invite personal contacts.

4. *Evangelism teams for prayer and follow-up of prospects.* Invite a select group of committed brothers and sisters to meet regularly to track the progress of promising contacts. Keep a list of all visitors and prospects, with contact information and up-to-date progress reports. Pray together for each name on the list. Talk about what can be done to help the person take the next step. Encourage each other. When a positive development occurs with one of these prospects, send a text message to everyone on the team. Keep it ever before them. Talk about strategies for welcoming guests and following up with them when they show some interest.

Andrew Carnegie said, "It marks a big step in your development when you come to realize that other people can help you do a better job than you could do alone." Fostering a spirit of teamwork in evangelism can transform the culture of a congregation.

Teaching Suggestion: Start With Ecclesiastes

Success in evangelism is not curriculum-specific, as long as the truth of God is taught. Nonetheless, part of "handling accurately the word of truth" is knowing how to use the sword of the Spirit to penetrate the deep recesses where soul and spirit are divided, joints and marrow meet, and the thoughts and intentions of the heart are discerned (Hebrews 4:12; 2 Timothy 2:15). *I like to bait my hook with Ecclesiastes because it resonates with people and speaks to them universally, regardless of background.* I cover the following points as a one-session entrée to evangelism:

+ The Cyclical Nature of Life — Ecclesiastes 1:1-11
+ The Emptiness of Worldly Preoccupations — Ecclesiastes 2:1-11
+ The Inescapable Conclusion — Ecclesiastes 12:1-8, 13-14

The compelling conclusion is that this life is a probationary period for a day of reckoning, beyond which we will be rewarded or punished:

"The end of the matter; all has been heard. Fear God and keep his commandments, for this is the whole duty of man. For God will bring every deed into judgment, with every secret thing, whether good or evil" (Ecclesiastes 12:13-14).

I often use the following illustration: Toward the end of his life, the famous scientist Carl Sagan wrote a book called Pale Blue Dot. Beginning on the first page, he alludes to a Voyager spacecraft that was projected billions of miles into space. In the photographic images sent back to earth, our planet appears to be nothing more than a "pale blue dot"—hence the title of the book. Mr. Sagan argues that we think that what we're accomplishing here is important, but it's really not. We're nothing but ant-like creatures on a "pale blue dot" in a vast universe so big that it staggers the imagination. Moreover, he argues that there is no one *out there* to save us from ourselves.

If you take God and Judgment Day out of the equation, he's absolutely right. However, if God and Judgment Day really exist, he's dead wrong! If life on earth is a probationary period, then everything we do counts, and we're playing for keeps. Our lives in the latter case are of tremendous worth and value, and eternity hangs in the balances. Consequently, we need *God* and *Judgment Day* to validate our purpose here on earth. If you take them away, then our lives are not worth very much at all! Our inherent worth and value are inextricably tied to an ultimate *day of reckoning* with God.

Most unbelievers haven't thought much about the preceding point, and when I make it, it hits them over the head like a ton of lead. Then I make the point that not only do we need God, he has not left us without direction and purpose: *"fear God and keep his commandments, for this is the whole duty of man."* The God who grants you life and breath has invested your life with infinite purpose and meaning, and He cares enough about us to reveal a *blueprint* for living. Whether or not we take advantage of this opportunity is of vital importance.

When this point is made forcefully but lovingly, the typical response of unbelievers is, "Tell me more."

Teaching The Gospel … Building Faith

There are many specific approaches to teaching the gospel to lost souls, and a multitude of aids, charts, books, and multi-media tools is available. I like to use the Gospel of Luke to build people's faith, and then follow up with Acts to show them how faith responds to the gospel message. Whatever approach you decide to use, remember that the gospel encompasses three essential points:

+ People are lost in sin (Romans 3:10, 23)
+ Salvation is by the grace of God (Romans 6:23; Ephesians 2:8-9)
+ This grace is accessed by obedient faith (John 3:16; Hebrews 5:9; Matthew 7:21; Acts 2:38)

Your role as an evangelist is to build people's faith to the point that they must respond in obedience. "So faith comes from hearing, and hearing through the word of Christ" (Romans 10:17). Biblical faith involves three sub-components:

+ Conviction of mind (which comes through evidence) Hebrews 11:1; John 20:30-31
+ Trust of heart (which develops through a growing awareness of the trustworthiness of the Lord and His promises) Romans 4:20-21
+ Surrender of the will (which results from an acceptance of the conditions of salvation) Luke 17:5-10; Hebrews 5:9

Whatever methods and scriptures you utilize to teach people about God and His plan of salvation, your goal is to gently build conviction of mind, trust of heart, and surrender of the will. The more you work with people with this paradigm in mind, the more you will see deficiencies that need to be addressed in the conversion process. Patience is essential.

Pressing For A Decision

After years of doing this work, I can usually tell when prospects are getting close. Their level of interest rises. There is a new intensity. The questions they ask take on more urgency. The light bulb goes on, and it becomes painfully obvious that they need the remedy that only the Savior Jesus can provide. Even the oft-cited conditions of salvation in Acts 2:38 are a response to those who were "cut to the heart," saying, "Brothers, what shall we do?" (2:37).

I do not believe you have to *sell* the gospel or press hard for a commitment until a person is adequately "taught" (John 6:44-45). On the other hand, when it becomes obvious that the word of God performs its "work" in a believer (1 Thessalonians 2:13) and an honest seeker is getting close, then one should proceed with urgency. The question of Ananias to Saul of Tarsus is on target: "And now why do you wait? Rise and be baptized and wash away your sins, calling on his name" (Acts 22:16).

Follow-Up And Integration

When someone is baptized into Christ, and a new brother or sister is welcomed into the family of God, the local church is charged with excitement. Members should be challenged and motivated to go find someone else to teach. However, in the midst of the enthusiasm, one should not forget the vulnerability of this new babe in Christ. In so many respects, the work has just begun.

If winning a soul is part of a team effort, chances are greater that *keeping* him will be part of a team effort. His brothers and sisters in Christ must make a personal investment in integrating him into the local church family. If there is a group in the church specifically devoted to teamwork in welcoming new members, there will be less of a chance for babes to "fall through the cracks." I also emphasize the need of follow-up in teaching. Once again, there are many approaches. I have developed a 12-lesson program called, "Your First Steps."

One of the great thrills of my life has been nurturing the faith of people who were outside of Christ, and seeing them grow to become strong Christians. It is especially rewarding to witness such a one bringing *someone else* to the Lord, but it is not altogether rare. When a deep-seated evangelistic awareness becomes part of the DNA of a congregation, momentum is built and conversions may come in spurts. Our job as evangelists is to patiently teach, encourage, and facilitate, "that we may present everyone mature in Christ" (Colossians 1:28). Paul adds a footnote to this wonderful sentiment: "For this I toil, struggling with all his energy that he powerfully works within me" (1:29).

When and How to Move
By Harold Hancock

I have preached for forty-two years. During this time I have moved four times. I stayed three and a half years at my first work, a little over four years at my second work, nine and a half years at my third work, and I have just finished my twenty-fifth year at my fourth work. My tenure with these churches may be more of a testament to the goodness and patience of the members of these churches than to my abilities as a preacher, but I have been blessed in the works that I have done and the moves I have made. Though I am not so naïve as to think that there has never been anyone in these congregations who wanted me to move, I have never been asked to move by any of the churches that I served. I am not sure how qualified this makes me to discuss "When and How to Move," but it is my assignment. I trust that the things I share with you from my knowledge of the Scriptures, the research I have done on the subject, the insight I have gained through my own limited experiences, and some of the observations I have made from the lives and experiences of fellow-preachers will help you exercise sound judgment if you contemplate moving.

I read that preachers for the church move on the average of once every three years. I cannot attest to the accuracy of the statement. My own thoughts and observations lead me to believe that in more recent years the attitudes of preachers and churches have changed; many preachers desire to stay and work with a church for longer periods of time, and many churches are not disposed to change preachers needlessly. Still, we must admit that most preachers will move from time to time— some more frequently than others. Some preachers are asked or told to move by the church for which they preach; some preachers choose to move, much to the dismay and regrets of the church for which they preach; sometimes the decision to move is mutual—both the preacher and the church agree it is time for a change. God gives no specific instructions in the Scriptures about preachers moving; therefore, when, and if, preachers move is a matter of judgment. Such decisions should be made prayerfully; divine principles and "wisdom that is from above" (James 3:17) should guide preachers in their decisions about moving, just as the teachings of the Scriptures and the proper applications of Scripture should influence our decisions in every matter—"whatever you do in word or deed, do all in the name of the Lord Jesus" (Colossians 3:17).

The book of Acts furnishes us with a thirty-year snapshot of the early church; in it we find a few examples of preachers working with churches and observe their stay among them. Paul and Barnabas remained in Antioch and taught for a year (Acts 11:26) before being chosen by the Holy Spirit for a different work (Acts 13:1-4). Paul spent a year and a half in Corinth (Acts 18:11) and three years in Ephesus (Acts 20:31). Luke possibly spent six years in Philippi. This is deduced by carefully watching the pronouns, "we" and "they," as Luke writes Acts. Luke came to Philippi with Paul (Acts 16:16), but did not leave with him (Acts 16:40). He rejoined Paul when Paul returned to Philippi and left for Troas (Acts 20:6). Furthermore, Philip went to Caesarea shortly after the conversion of the Ethiopian eunuch (Acts 8:40). Twenty years later the Scriptures speak again of "Philip the evangelist;" he had a house and was still in Caesarea (Acts 21:8). These preachers' stays with the churches were not decided on a whim or by selfish ambitions. They made their decisions for the good of the cause of Christ and according to their commissions, opportunities, effectiveness, and circumstances. *The cause of Christ should always be foremost in preachers' minds when trying to decide when to move,* but opportunities, effectiveness, and circumstances will also continue to be determining factors in preachers' decisions.

Consider some of the things that may affect your decision to move or not to move:

The Spiritual Condition Of Churches

God desires that churches grow, and He gave preachers to help them do so (Ephesians 4:11-12). Preachers and churches have to determine who fits where best and for how long. If you determine that you have done your best work for a church and that someone else could now be more helpful, it is time to consider moving. However, be careful; do not be too rash in making such decisions. Most works have their ups, downs, and plateaus. Do not make a permanent decision on the temporary condition of a church. You may also ask yourself what the next preacher must do to revitalize church growth. You may discover that you may need to be more diligent or to redirect some of your gospel efforts to regain your effectiveness. Sometimes, changing ourselves may be better for us, our families, and the church than changing works.

You know that it is time to move when the elders or "church leaders" come and ask you to move. This may be a bit disconcerting, especially if you did not see the decision coming or do not think it is a good decision. Yet, many preachers have been told, "We like you, and we think you are doing a good job, but we think it is time for change." Remember that it is a judgment call, and one that the church has a right to make. The decision may inconvenience you and your family, but accept it graciously. Do not allow yourself to become embittered (Ephesians 4:31); do nothing to harm the body of Christ, such as encouraging or allowing division to ensue for your personal gain or to stoke your ego. Do not needlessly destroy your relationship with these brethren. Time may prove their decision to be wise for them and good for you.

Your Own Spiritual Condition

As a preacher you may need to move for your own or your family's spiritual welfare or growth. Some churches are "dead" (Revelation 3:1) and some are "lukewarm" (Revelation 3:15-16). If you cannot resurrect or revitalize them through gospel efforts, they may become a detriment to your happiness and spiritual well-being or a threat to your family's spirituality; it may be time to move. Just make sure you have given a good effort in contending earnestly for the faith (Jude 1:3) and defending the gospel (Philippians 1:17) before you decide to leave.

All may be well with you and with the church for which you preach, but you may feel a need to "get out of your comfort zone" so you can grow; perhaps you do not presently work under the oversight of elders, but yearn for the opportunity to do so. You may cherish the idea of having a backlog of sermons and classes and experiences to draw from while you restudy and rework some of your older lessons and prepare new ones. You may determine that you are particularly suited for another work that comes available and choose to move. A new work with new challenges may stimulate you to greater growth. When moving to a new work, be careful not to rely entirely on past labors and accomplishments; you must continue to be a good steward of the word of God—"Be diligent to present yourself approved to God, a worker who does not need to be ashamed, rightly dividing the word of truth" (2 Timothy 2:15).

Family Matters

Most of us are not alone—we come from families and have families. There may be times when your family will dictate the need for a move, the place you locate, or the size of work you undertake. You may choose to relocate close to aging family members and pursue a less demanding work so you can be there for them when they need you. You may wish to work with a congregation that has couples your own age or young people the age of your children. The community you will be a part of and the schools your children will attend may be a big consideration in your move. You may need to "think twice" about making an unnecessary move and uprooting your family from familiar territory. I was blessed and moved only once after my kids reached school age, but I found that while

I had little adjusting to do because my world revolved mostly around the church, my children's adjustment was harder; they had to adjust not only to a new church but to new schools and new friends at school. It was a good day when my oldest son jokingly told me he had forgiven me for moving him as he was about to enter the ninth grade and admitted it was a good move for all of us. Remember, your decision to move or not to move affects more than just you—the whole family is very much involved with the consequences of your decisions.

Money

Some churches, though hopefully they are few and far between, want to keep their preacher "humble"—they want him to be paid no more than what the lowest paid member receives—even if the preacher's financial responsibilities are greater. Some preachers never receive raises in pay—not even a "cost of living" raise. If these things happen to you, you can become discouraged. You may feel your work is not appreciated by the brethren or that moving is the only way to take care of your family and gain financial peace. Perhaps you are adequately paid, but another church offers you an opportunity to come work with them at a greater income. Should you accept just on the basis of money?

"The Lord has commanded that those who preach the gospel should live by the gospel" (1 Corinthians 9:14). Brethren should be taught this and expected to obey this command as much so as any of the commandments of the Lord (James 2:10). As a preacher, you have an obligation to provide for your family, as do other Christians (1 Timothy 5:8). You cannot ignore these truths nor neglect your God-given obligations. However, you must beware of covetousness (Luke 12:13-15). Paul's life exemplified his pure motives for preaching the gospel (1 Thessalonians 2:9). Yours must do the same. You must learn and practice contentment (1 Timothy 6:6-10; Philippians 4:11-13).

Remember, also, you would be just as wrong to remain with a church because of a good income when it is evident that the cause of

Christ is being hindered by your stay as you would be to leave and go elsewhere out of covetousness. Though money will sometimes enter your considerations when moving, it must not be the only or greatest concern in your decision.

If you carefully monitor your opportunities, effectiveness, and circumstances, and "keep your finger on the pulse" of the congregation for which you preach and on your own spiritual needs, you may sense when the time for a move is drawing near. If you do perceive that a move is in the "not so distant future," do not wait until time runs out or until your relationship with the church for which you preach deteriorates. Looking ahead and deciding to move before you are asked to may keep you from becoming desperate; it will give you time to carefully select a good church to work with—one where the cause of Christ will be served. When possible, it is far better to leave a church on good terms and with the members of the church desiring that you stay longer than leaving on bad terms and with most of its members glad to see you go.

There are things you should keep in mind as you search for a new church:

* *Be honest with yourself, the church you are with, and the church that is considering you.*

There are always churches looking for preachers and preachers looking for churches. Churches may contact you just to see if you might be interested in moving. However, if churches know you are looking to move, you will likely have several contact you. It may be that you know of churches looking for a preacher, and you desire to contact one or more of them. I do not think you are obligated to inform the church you are with every time you are contacted by another church and asked to consider a new work. However, if you are actively seeking to move, do not hide this from the church for which you preach; you would not want them to be actively looking for another preacher without telling you. Furthermore, do not waste the time and money of churches by "trying out" for them if you have no inclination in moving to work with them; do not view it as an opportunity for an "extra paycheck" or a paid vacation. To do such cheapens preaching and is a waste of the Lord's money.

- *Remember that preachers are not in competition with one another and neither are churches of Christ.*

Some churches have "preacher parades"; they "try out" numerous preachers, committing to no one until they hear and talk to all of them. They then choose the one they want. This does not seem to be a good method of selecting a preacher. This encourages preachers to vie against one another; it leaves preachers in limbo for a period of time; and it can cause division in the church—part of the church may want one preacher while others in the church want another. Who wants to start a new work knowing some do not want you to be their preacher? You are better off to seek the church's decision after they have heard you preach, talked with you, and reflected on your abilities and before they consider anyone else. If they are unwilling to do so, this is not the place for you.

In the same manner, as a preacher, do not talk to multiple churches, committing to none, but turning down none in hopes of receiving a "better offer." If you doubt a work is the right work for you, turn it down and look elsewhere.

- *Find out as much as you can about the church that you are considering before deciding on the work; know what they expect of you and let them know your expectations of them.*

Talk with any of your friends who may know of the church and its history. Do they think it is a strong church or a church with potential? If possible, find out why the previous preacher left. Were there problems that caused him to leave? This may tell you volumes about the church. Talk with the leaders of the church. Are you agreed on doctrinal issues and present day controversies? Make sure you are agreed on the support you will be receiving, the work you will be doing, the time that is allotted to you for gospel meetings and vacation, etc. Any matters that are important to you or to them need to be discussed fully before agreeing on the work. You do not want to move and then find disturbing differences.

You will likely maintain close friends from your former work and stay in contact with some of the members of that church. Having invested your time and efforts in the church you left behind, you will naturally remain interested in it; you should want to see them grow. Do not allow your interest and concern to turn into meddling. Do not try to exert an inordinate influence on the work. It will only hinder the work of their new preacher and cause trouble for the church. Furthermore, do not spend time second guessing your decision to move or looking back with longing eyes. The decision has been made. Work to make the new work a good work.

Determining when to move is a matter of judgment. You can talk with other preachers, church leaders, church members, and read what some have written for counsel, but, ultimately, it is a decision that has to be made by you or the church. It is a decision that affects you, your family, and your work for the Lord. It should be made prayerfully and with a love for the cause of Christ at heart and with wisdom from above. May God bless you in your work in the kingdom and in the decisions you have to make.

Dear Young Preacher
From Harold E. Turner

*If the job of preaching the gospel was being done only
by those of absolute perfection, the field of
preachers would be reduced to zero.*

To a dear young man who has dedicated his life early on to the proclamation of the gospel of Christ, are these few thoughts earnestly dedicated with the hope of adding some meaningful thing to the greatest work that can possibly be done.

Don't forget to study and read for yourself. It can be a rather shocking event when all of a sudden you are faced with the preparation of a couple of sermons a week, two or three classes, a bulletin and other things to be done, and if caution isn't used, you can wind up reading and studying for presentations while forgetting about self-nourishment and that which is necessary to your own spiritual survival. This is not to say the other materials and preparation will not be of help to you, but there is no substitute, when all is said and done, for just reading with you in mind. See to it well.

Preparation is the key to satisfaction. There is absolutely no substitute for it, and without it your work will not be as efficient as it should be, people who hear will not receive what they have a right to hear and then, at the end of the day, you will be left with an empty feeling of a job half-way and poorly done. In this you will experience no joy, accomplish less than you should, displease the Lord you serve, and fail in honoring the work you have chosen to do. And you will not be satisfied with the job done! Prepare thoroughly and then do it right.

Don't take to the pulpit that which should be dealt with one-on-one. There are private matters that need to be dealt with on a private basis;

there are also problems that demand a public exposure or discussion or topics that are pulpit worthy. Learn to distinguish between the two categories and act wisely concerning the same. My father, L. K. Turner, advised me long years ago of these concerns, and the advice is needed by all who would endeavor to do the work of preaching and teaching. It is a form of cowardice to beat someone over the head publicly when I should be talking to him face to face.

Decide Sunday night before going to bed what you will preach next Sunday. If you are not careful, you can waste big chunks of time just trying to decide what to discuss next. That may not happen for a while, but before too long you will have exhausted your store house of ideas, preached everything you have ever thought of or heard about, and then it easily can become panic crazy time trying like everything to decide topics for next Sunday (which Sundays will seem to come about every other day), and the cute little saying, "There is nothing that will inspire a sermon like the setting of the sun on Saturday evening." will be small comfort. Before going to bed each Sunday night, decide what you will start working on Monday morning. To do so will greatly assist your work load, your week, the end product, and your sanity.

Remember your family. With the passing of time, the increasing feelings of responsibility regarding work with the local church, opportunities to hold meetings elsewhere, articles to write and work that needs generally to be done and never seems to end, can become a problem that needs its proper attention too. As your work grows (and it will) so it will be with your family and the everyday needs and duties that attach to that. The proper balance between the two needs to be found and the one taken as seriously as the other. To preach to the whole world and lose your own family is a sad thing and need not be if that balance is remembered. So, remember it.

Give no occasion for brethren to feel taken advantage of. One of the worst feelings you can give to another or others is that you are taking advantage of them or the prevailing circumstance. This feeling can result from preachers playing golf five days a week or by showing up ill-prepared for work to be done in classes or pulpit (and don't think for a minute they will not notice when that is the case), or by not dealing responsibly with financial demands. Learn to live within your means. Pay your bills. And if you happen to be involved in "outside support," send detailed and full reports regularly of finances received and work done. The "my income is my business and none of theirs" is so transparent that it reeks of what it is, an obvious attempt to hide the full truth. It ought not be so. Keep things open and above board and it will work to the good of all.

Don't let your own short-comings blow you out of the water. Realistically speaking, you are going to make some mistakes along the way. Some will be more serious than others, but they will be there to whatever degree. This is not to justify wrong, excuse serious sins committed, or to encourage looseness toward bad behavior, but it is still so that sooner or later problems will arise and good judgment will fail. As the occasion demands, make wrongs right. Say, "I'm sorry, forgive me." Meet the conditions of forgiveness and then get on with it the best way you can. Learn from mistakes made, grow with the process and don't let the fact you are less than perfect cause the attitude of despair. *If the job of preaching the gospel was being done only by those of absolute perfection, the field of preachers would be reduced to zero.*

When you become a piece of sheetrock, learn to deal with it. In any "new work" you will go through that renowned "honeymoon stage" during which period all will be great and wonderful, you will be cousin to the greats of the pulpit, loved and appreciated by just about all who attend and heaven on earth will exist—*for a time.* Then things will settle to a more down-to-earth reality, the critics will appear with a degree of boldness, listeners (some, anyway) will participate with a less attentive ear, babies will be taken out only after the doors and windows have shaken thoroughly, and you will gradually begin to feel more and more like sheetrock on the wall or carpet on the floor. Now, it's time to go to work with even more interest, zeal, and determination to have something to say that needs to be said and that is worth hearing. As your efforts are renewed to be what you have pledged yourself to be, it will be amazing how the sheetrock feeling will fade away and how much good there is still left to do.

Do not form the habit of being selective about meetings giving preference to the "fat" ones. To the doing of good you are dedicated, and it is difficult to measure such matters ahead of time. You may go to the big place, stay for a time and then look back upon said experience wishing it had never happened. On the other hand that small, seemingly insignificant meeting may turn out in truth to be full of all kinds of good things in the gospel, and what seemed in the outset to be of meager potential may be one of the best preaching events of your life. To try to put dollars and cents value on such things is a colossal mistake and, to say the least, demeans the work you have set before you. Take the opportunities as they come and do the best you can with all.

A sense of humor really does help. It really does! Some things will tend to over-emphasis and be given time and attention not deserved. As is opposed to the brain-wrenching category, they just simply deserve to be laughed off, period. On one occasion after doing the best I knew how in a class on John 6, a brother in all seriousness abruptly stated, "Brother Turner, I don't think we can be too dogmatic about the miraculous being involved there in the feeding of the 5,000, because we don't know the size of those fish." Was it appropriate at that point to spend the next three sessions giving expression to the unlikelihood of a small lad dragging all over the hills of Palestine a couple of killer whales or perhaps better to laugh it off and continue with the class? Another brother, after praying for my "ready recollection" (for which prayer I am becoming increasingly thankful) added to it all, "and help us while he does his work to have itching ears." Did he deserve to be berated for 30 minutes or were we all right in just laughing it off (to ourselves of course)? After all, I have said a few stupid things along the way and probably will add to the list before it's all over. A good sense of humor really does help.

Learn to attach the seat of your pants to a chair. For this there is no substitute. Whether or not you are willing to do this will determine by and large whether or not your work as a gospel preacher is going to be rich and fulfilling to you and others or whether it will involve a shallowness from the outset, from which you will never be able to detach yourself—thus spending your preaching life striving for some degree of appropriateness within the limits of said shallowness. Attach the seat of your pants to a chair!

Learn to take criticism. It will come your way. It should come your way, for it is just a stubborn truth that every now and then we really do have it coming, and the fellow who thinks that isn't so has an inflated opinion of himself that probably only he entertains. But we have to educate ourselves into this one—*we have to decide ahead of time the attitude we will have when the criticism comes.* Some are unjustified. Some are needed and will help greatly in the work set before us. Be wise in this regard too.

Develop your own way (style) of doing things. You can do something that nobody else on earth can do, and that is to be the best you you can possibly be in proclaiming the gospel. Early on you will hear others you greatly admire and appreciate and will probably desire to emulate. That's natural. But you do not want to be a cheap counterfeit of another. Let your personality, inclinations, and natural ways have their place—develop your own style and things will flow more easily and effectively. Learn from the other fellow but do not become the other fellow.

Understand you have the potential for accomplishing in the lives of many the highest order of good. There are different degrees and kinds of "good" that can be done for others, but the greatest good you will ever do anybody is to take some aspect of the will of the Father, communicate it unto him, help him to see it as it is, and challenge his thinking to application. It is this understanding that will help put all the lumps, bumps, problems, junk, and stuff associated with the work in proper place and create the determination to persevere come what may. May our Father bless you now and always young man as you start the journey you have chosen, most precious indeed.

www.ingramcontent.com/pod-product-compliance
Lightning Source LLC
Chambersburg PA
CBHW031959040426

42448CB00006B/422